Psychotherapy Classics

Landmark Articles in the History of Psychotherapy and Counseling

ALBERT BANDURA

ALBERT ELLIS

CARL ROGERS

DAVID ROSENTHAL & JEROME D. FRANK

LAURANCE SHAFFER

THOMAS SZASZ

ISBN-10: 1491022353

ISBN-13: 978-1491022351

CONTENTS

A WORD FROM THE EDITOR

This wonderful collection of articles originally published between 1946 and 1961 has been put together as part of an initiative to make important, insightful and engaging psychology publications widely available. Written by some of the most influential and enigmatic thinkers of the 20th century each article is an essential read for anybody with an interest in the history and development of psychotherapy and counseling.

About The Editor

David Webb has a first class honors degree in psychology and a Masters in Occupational psychology. For a number of years, he was a lecturer in psychology at the University of Huddersfield (UK).

He is the writer and host of four websites built around his teaching and research interests. Together these websites receive over 120,000 unique visitors each month and generate over 4 million yearly page views.

www.all-about-psychology.com

www.all-about-forensic-psychology.com

www.all-about-forensic-science.com

www.all-about-body-language.com

An active promoter of psychology through social media his psychology facebook page (www.facebook.com/psychologyonline) has over 90,000 followers and he is listed by The British Psychological Society among the top psychologists who tweet (@psych101.) His most recent publication, The Incredibly Interesting Psychology Book (www.amazon.com/dp/B00CR1DX22) is an international #1 Best Seller.

1. SIGNIFICANT ASPECTS OF CLIENT-CENTERED THERAPY

(Carl Rogers 1946)

In this landmark publication Carl Rogers outlines the origins of client-centered therapy, the process of client-centered therapy, the discovery and capacity of the client and the client-centered nature of the therapeutic relationship.

In planning to address this group, I have considered and discarded several possible topics. I was tempted to describe the process of non-directive therapy and the counselor techniques and procedures which seem most useful in bringing about this process. But much of this material is now in writing. My own book on counseling and psychotherapy contains much of the basic material, and my recent more popular book on counseling with returning servicemen tends to supplement it. The philosophy of the client-centered approach and its application to work with children is persuasively presented by Allen. The application to counseling of industrial employees is discussed in the volume by Cantor. Curran has now published in book form one of the several research studies which are throwing new light on both process and procedure. Axline is publishing a book on play and group therapy. Snyder is bringing out a book of cases. So it seems unnecessary to come a long distance to summarize material which is, or soon will be obtainable in written form.

Another tempting possibility, particularly in this setting, was to discuss some of the roots from which the client-centered approach has sprung. It would have been interesting to show how in its concepts of repression and release, in its stress upon catharsis and insight, it has many roots in Freudian thinking, and to acknowledge that indebtedness. Such an analysis could also have shown that in its concept of the individual's ability to organize his own experience there is an even deeper indebtedness to the work of Rank, Taft, and

Allen. In its stress upon objective research, the subjecting of fluid attitudes to scientific investigation, the willingness to submit all hypotheses to a verification or disproof by research methods, the debt is obviously to the whole field of American psychology, with its genius for scientific methodology. It could also have been pointed out that although everyone in the clinical field has been heavily exposed to the eclectic "team" approach to therapy of the child guidance movement, and the somewhat similar eclecticism of the Adolf Meyers - Hopkins school of thought, these eclectic viewpoint have perhaps not been so fruitful in therapy and that little from these sources has been retained in the non-directive approach. It might also have been pointed out that in its basic trend away from guiding and directing the client. the non-directive approach is deeply rooted in practical clinical experience, and is in accord with the experience of most clinical workers, so much so that one of the commonest reactions of experienced therapists is that "You have crystallized and put into words something that I have been groping toward in my own experience for a long time."

Such an analysis, such a tracing or root ideas, needs to be made, but I doubt my own ability to make it. I am also doubtful that anyone who is deeply concerned with a new development knows with any degree of accuracy where his ideas came from.

Consequently I am, in this presentation. Adopting a third pathway. While I shall bring in a brief description of process and procedure. and while I shall acknowledge in a general way our indebtedness to many root sources, and shall recognize the many common elements shared by client-centered therapy and other approaches, I believe it will be to our mutual advantage if I stress primarily those aspects in which nondirective therapy differs most sharply and deeply from other therapeutic procedures. I hope to point out some of the basically significant ways in which the client-centered viewpoint differs from others, not only in its present principles, but in the wider divergencies which are implied by the projection of its central principles.

THE PREDICTABLE PROCESS OF CLIENT-CENTERED THERAPY

The first of the three distinctive elements of client-centered therapy to which I wish to call your attention is the predictability of the therapeutic process in this approach. We find, both clinically and statistically, that a predictable pattern of therapeutic development takes place. The assurance which we feel about this was brought home to me recently when I played a recorded first interview for the graduate students in our practicum immediately after it was recorded, pointing out the characteristic aspects, and agreeing to play later interviews for them to let them see the later phases of the counseling process. The fact that I knew with assurance what the later pattern would be before it had occurred only struck me as I thought about the incident. We have become clinically so accustomed to this predictable quality that we take it for granted. Perhaps a brief summarized description of this therapeutic process will indicate those elements of which we feel sure.

It may be said that we now know how to initiate a complex and predictable chain of events in dealing with the maladjusted individual, a chain of events which is therapeutic, and which operates effectively in problem situations of the most diverse type. This predictable chain of events may come about through the use of language as in counseling, through symbolic language, as in play therapy, through disguised language as in drama or puppet therapy. It is effective in dealing with individual situations, and also in small group situations.

It is possible to state with some exactness the conditions which must be met in order to initiate and carry through this releasing therapeutic experience. Below are listed in brief form the conditions which seem to be necessary, and the therapeutic results which occur.

This experience which releases the growth forces within the

individual will come about in most cases if the following elements are present.

1. If the counselor operates on the principle that the individual is basically responsible for himself, and is willing for the individual to keep that responsibility.

2. If the counselor operates on the principle that the client has a strong drive to become mature, socially adjusted. independent, productive, and relies on this force, not on his own powers, for therapeutic change.

3. If the counselor creates a warm and permissive atmosphere in which the individual is free to bring out any attitudes and feelings which he may have, no matter how unconventional, absurd, or contradictory these attitudes may be. The client is as free to withhold expression as he is to give expression to his feelings.

4. If the limits which are set are simple limits set on behavior, and not limits set on attitudes. (This applies mostly to children. The child may not be permitted to break a window or leave the room. but he is free to feel like breaking a window, and the feeling is fully accepted. The adult client may not be permitted more than an hour for an interview, but there is full acceptance of his desire to claim more time.)

5. If the therapist uses only those procedures and techniques in the interview which convey his deep understanding of the emotionalized attitudes expressed and his acceptance of them. This understanding is perhaps best conveyed by a sensitive reflection and clarification of the client's attitudes. The counselor's acceptance involves neither approval nor disapproval.

6. If the counselor refrains from any expression or action which is contrary to the preceding principles. This means reframing from questioning, probing, blame, interpretation, advice, suggestion,

persuasion, reassurance If these conditions are met. then it may be said with assurance that in the great majority of cases the following results will take place.

1. The client will express deep and motivating attitudes.

2. The client will explore his own attitudes and reactions more fully than he has previously done and will come to be aware of aspects of his attitudes which he has previously denied.

3. He will arrive at a clearer conscious realization of his motivating attitudes and will accept himself more completely. This realization and this acceptance will include attitudes previously denied. He may or may not verbalize this clearer conscious understanding of himself and his behavior.

4. In the light of his clearer perception of himself he will choose, on his own initiative and on his own responsibility, new goal which are more satisfying than his maladjusted goals.

5. He will choose to behave in a different fashion in order to reach these goals, and this new behavior will be in the direction of greater psychological growth and maturity. It will also be more spontaneous and less tense, more in harmony with social needs of others, will represent a more realistic and more comfortable adjustment to life. It will be more integrated than his former behavior. It will be a step forward in the life of the individual.

The best scientific description of this process is that supplied by Snyder. Analyzing a number of cases with strictly objective research techniques, Snyder has discovered that the development in these cases is roughly parallel, that the initial phase of catharsis is replaced by a phase in which insight becomes the most significant element, and this in turn by a phase marked by the increase in positive choice and action

Clinically, we know that sometimes this process is relatively shallow, involving primarily a fresh reorientation to an immediate problem, and in other instances so deep as to involve a complete reorientation of personality. It is recognizably the same process whether it involves a girl who is unhappy in a dormitory and is able in three interviews to see something of her childishness and dependence, and to take steps in a mature direction, or whether it involves a young man who is on the edge of a schizophrenic break, and who in thirty interviews works out deep insights in relation to his desire for his father's death, and his possessive and incestuous impulses toward is mother, and who not only takes new steps but rebuilds his whole personality in the process. Whether shallow or deep, it is basically the same.

We are coming to recognize with assurance characteristic aspects of each phase of the process. We know that the catharsis involves a gradual and more complete expression of emotionalized attitudes. We know that characteristically the conversation goes from superficial problems and attitudes to deeper problems and attitudes. We know that this process of exploration gradually unearths relevant attitudes which have been denied to consciousness. We recognize too that the process of achieving insight is likely to involve more adequate facing of reality as it exists within the self, as well as external reality; that it involves the relating of problems to each other, the perception of patterns of behavior; that it involves the acceptance of hitherto denied elements of the self, and a reformulating of the self-concept; and that it involves the making of new plans.

In the final phase we know that the choice of new ways of behaving will be in conformity with the newly organized concept of the self; that first steps in putting these plans into action will be small but symbolic; that the individual will feel only a minimum degree of confidence that he can put his plans into effect, that later steps implement more and more completely the new concept of self, and that this process continues beyond the conclusion of the therapeutic interviews.

If these statements seem to contain too much assurance, to sound "too good to be true," I can only say that for many of them we now have research backing, and that as rapidly as possible we are developing our research to bring all phases of the process under objective scrutiny. Those of us working clinically with client-centered therapy regard this predictability as a settled characteristic, even though we recognize that additional research will be necessary to fill out the picture more completely.

It is the implication of this predictability which is startling. Whenever, in science, a predictable process has been discovered, it has been found possible to use it as a starting point for a whole chain of discoveries. We regard this as not only entirely possible, but inevitable, with regard to this predictable process in therapy. Hence, we regard this orderly and predictable nature of nondirective therapy as one of its most distinctive and significant points of difference from other approaches. Its importance lies not only in the fact that it is a present difference. but in the fact that it points toward a sharply different future, in which scientific exploration of this known chain of events should lead to many new discoveries, developments. and applications.

THE DISCOVERY OF THE CAPACITY OF THE CLIENT

Naturally the question is raised, what is the reason for this predictability in a type of therapeutic procedure in which the therapist serves only a catalytic function? Basically the reason for the predictability of the therapeutic process lies in the discovery - and I use that word intentionally - that within the client reside constructive forces whose strength and uniformity have been either entirely unrecognized or grossly underestimated. It is the clear-cut and disciplined reliance by the therapist upon those forces within the client, which seems to account for the orderliness of the therapeutic process, and its consistency from one client to the next.

I mentioned that I regarded this as a discovery. I would like to amplify that statement. We have known for centuries that catharsis and emotional release were helpful. Many new methods have been and are being developed to bring about release, but the principle is not new. Likewise, we have known since Freud's time that insight, if it is accepted and assimilated by the client, is therapeutic. The principle is not new. Likewise we have realized that revised action patterns, new ways of behaving, may come about as a result of insight. The principle is not new.

But we have not known or recognized that in most if not all individuals there exist growth forces, tendencies toward self-actualization, which may act as the sole motivation for therapy. We have not realized that under suitable psychological conditions these forces bring about emotional release in those areas and at those rates which are most beneficial to the individual. These forces drive the individual to explore his own attitudes and his relationship to reality. and to explore these areas effectively. We have not realized that the individual is capable of exploring his attitudes and feelings, including those which have been denied to consciousness, at a rate which does not cause panic, and to the depth required for comfortable adjustment. The individual is capable of discovering and perceiving, truly and spontaneously, the interrelationships between his own attitudes, and the relationship of himself to reality. The individual has the capacity and the strength to devise, quite unguided, the steps which will lead him to a more mature and more comfortable relationship to his reality. It is the gradual and increasing recognition of these capacities within the individual by the client-centered therapist that rates, I believe, the term discovery. All of these capacities I have described are released in the individual if a suitable psychological atmosphere is provided.

There has, of course, been lip service paid to the strength of the client, and the need of utilizing the urge toward independence which exists in the client. Psychiatrists, analysts, and especially social case workers have stressed this point. Yet it is clear from what is said, and even more clear from the case material cited. that this confidence is a very limited confidence. It is a confidence that the client can take over, if guided by the expert, a confidence that the client can assimilate insight if it is first, given to him by the expert, can make choices providing guidance is given at crucial points. It is, in short, the same sort of attitude which the mother has toward the adolescent. that she believes in his capacity to make his own decisions and guide his own life, providing he takes the directions of which she approves.

This is very evident in the latest book on psychoanalysis by Alexander and French. Although many of the former views and practices of psychoanalysis are discarded, and the procedures are far more nearly in line with those of nondirective therapy, it is still the therapist who is definitely in control. He gives the insights. he is ready to guide at crucial points. Thus while the authors state that the aim of the therapist is to free the patient to develop his capacities, and to increase his ability to satisfy his needs in ways acceptable to himself and society; and while they speak of the basic conflict between competition and cooperation as one which the individual must settle for himself; and speak of the integration of new insight as a normal function of the ego, it is clear when they speak of procedures that they have no confidence that the client has the capacity to do any of these things. For in practice, "As soon as the therapist takes the more active role we advocate, systematic planning becomes imperative. In addition to the original decision as to the particular sort of strategy to be employed in the treatment of any case, we recommend the conscious use of various techniques in a flexible manner, shifting tactics to fit the particular needs of the moment. Among these modifications of the standard technique are; using not only the method of free association but interviews of a more direct character, manipulating the frequency of the interviews, giving directives to the patient concerning his daily life, employing interruptions of long or short duration in preparation for ending the treatment, regulating the transference relation-hip to meet the specific needs of the case, and making use of real-life experiences as an integral part of therapy". At least this leaves no doubt as to whether it is the client's or the therapist's hour; it is clearly the latter. The capacities which the client is to develop are clearly not to be developed in the therapeutic sessions.

The client-centered therapist stands at an opposite pole, both theoretically and practically. He has learned that the constructive forces in the individual can be trusted. and that the more deeply they are relied upon, the more deeply they are released. He has come to build his procedures upon these hypotheses, which are rapidly becoming established as facts; that the client knows the areas of concern which he is ready to explore; that the client is the best judge as to the most desirable frequency of interviews; that the client can lead the way more efficiently than the therapist into deeper concerns; that the client will protect himself from panic by ceasing to explore an area which is becoming too painful; that the client can and will uncover all the repressed elements which it is necessary to uncover in order to build a comfortable adjustment; that the client can achieve for himself far truer and more sensitive and accurate insights than can possibly be given to him; that the client is capable of translating these insights into constructive behavior which weigh his own needs and desires realistically against the demands of society; that the client knows when therapy is completed and he is ready to cope with life independently. Only one condition is necessary for all these forces to be released, and that is the proper psychological atmosphere between client and therapist.

Our case records and increasingly our research bear out these statements. One might suppose that there would be a generally favorable reaction to this discovery, since it amounts in effect to tapping great reservoirs of hitherto little-used energy. Quite the contrary is true, however, in professional groups. There is no other aspect of client-centered therapy which comes under such vigorous attack. It seems to be genuinely disturbing to many professional people to entertain the thought that this client upon whom they have been exercising their professional skill actually knows more about his inner psychological self than they can possibly know, and that he possesses constructive strengths which make the constructive push by the therapist seem puny indeed by comparison. The willingness fully to accept this strength of the client, with all the re-orientation of therapeutic procedure which it implies, is one of the ways in which client-centered therapy differs most sharply from other therapeutic approaches.

THE CLIENT-CENTERED NATURE OF THE THERAPEUTIC RELATIONSHIP

The third distinctive feature of this type of therapy is the character of the relationship between therapist and client. Unlike other therapies in which the skills of the therapist are to be exercised upon the client. in this approach the skills of the therapist are focused upon creating a psychological atmosphere in which the client can work. If the counselor can create a relationship permeated by warmth, understanding, safety from any type of attack, no matter how trivial, and basic acceptance of the person as he is, then the client will drop his natural defensiveness and use the situation. As we have puzzled over the characteristics of a successful therapeutic relationship, we have come to feel that the sense of communication is very important. If the client feels that he is actually communicating his present attitudes, superficial, confused, or conflicted as they may be, and that his communication is understood rather than evaluated in any way, then he is freed to communicate more deeply. A relationship in which the client thus feels that he is communicating is almost certain to be fruitful.

All of this means a drastic reorganization in the counselor's thinking, particularly if he has previously utilized other approaches. He gradually learns that the statement that the time is to be "the client's hour" means just that, and that his biggest task is to make it more and more deeply true.

Perhaps something of the characteristics of the relationship may be suggested by excerpts from a paper written by a young minister who has spent several months learning client-centered counseling procedures.

"Because the client-centered, nondirective counseling approach has been rather carefully defined and clearly illustrated, it gives the "Illusion of Simplicity." The technique seems deceptively easy to master. Then you begin to practice. A word is wrong here and there. You don't quite reflect feeling, but reflect content instead. It is difficult to handle questions; you are tempted to interpret. Nothing seems so serious that further practice won't correct it. Perhaps you are having trouble playing two roles - that of minister and that of counselor. Bring up the question in class and the matter is solved again with a deceptive ease. But these apparently minor errors and a certain woodenness of response seem exceedingly persistent. "Only gradually does it dawn that if the technique is true it demands a feeling of warmth. You begin to feel that the attitude is the thing. Every little word is not so important if you have the correct accepting and permissive attitude toward the client. So you bear down on the permissiveness and acceptance. You will permiss and accept and reflect the client, if it kills you!

But you still have those troublesome questions from the client. He simply doesn't know the next step. He asks you to give him a hint, some possibilities, after all you are expected to know something, else why is he here! As a minister, you ought to have some convictions about what people should believe, how they should act. As a counselor, you should know something about removing this obstacle - you ought to have the equivalent of the surgeon's knife and use it. Then you begin to wonder. The technique is good, but...does it go far enough! does it really work on clients? is it right to leave a person helpless, when you might show him the way out?

Here it seems to me is the crucial point. "Narrow is the gate" and hard the path from here on. So one else can give satisfying answers and even the instructors seem frustrating because they appear not to be helpful in your specific case. For here is demanded of you what no other person can do or point out - and that is to rigorously scrutinize yourself and your attitudes towards others. Do you believe that all people truly have a creative potential in them? That each person is a unique individual and that he alone can work out his own individuality? Or do you really believe that some persons are of "negative value" and others are weak and must be led and taught by "wiser," "stronger" people.

"You begin to see that there is nothing compartmentalized about this method of counseling. It is not just counseling, because it demands the most exhaustive, penetrating, and comprehensive consistency. In other methods you can shape tools, pick them up for use when you will. But when genuine acceptance and permissiveness are your tools it requires nothing less than the whole complete personality. And to grow oneself is the most demanding of all."

He goes on to discuss the notion that the counselor must be restrained and "self-denying." He concludes that this is a mistaken notion.

"Instead of demanding less of the counselor's personality in the situation, client-centered counseling in some ways demands more. It demands discipline, not restraint. It calls for the utmost in sensitivity, appreciative awareness. channeled and disciplined. It demands that the counselor put all he has of these precious qualities into the situation, but in a disciplined, refined manner. It is restraint only in the sense that the counselor does not express himself in certain areas that he may use himself in others.

"Even this is deceptive, however. It is not so much restraint in any area as it is a focusing, sensitizing one's energies and personality in the direction of an appreciative and understanding attitude."

As time has gone by we have come to put increasing stress upon the "client-centeredness" of the relationship, because it is more effective the more completely the counselor concentrates upon trying to understand the client as the client seems to himself. As I look back upon some of our earlier published cases - the case of Herbert Bryan in my book, or Snyder's case of Mr. M. - I realize that we have gradually dropped the vestiges of subtle directiveness which are all too evident in those cases. We have come to recognize that if we can provide understanding of the way the client seems to himself at this moment, he can do the rest. The therapist must lay aside his preoccupation with diagnosis and his diagnostic shrewdness, must discard his tendency to make professional evaluations, must cease his endeavors to formulate an accurate prognosis, must give up the temptation subtly to guide the individual, and must concentrate on one purpose only; that of providing deep understanding and acceptance of the attitudes consciously held at this moment by the client as he explores step by step into the dangerous areas which he has been denying to consciousness.

I trust it is evident from this description that this type of relationship can exist only if the counselor is deeply and genuinely able to adopt these attitudes. Client-centered counseling, if it is to be effective, cannot be a trick or a tool. It is not a subtle way of guiding the client while pretending to let him guide himself. To be effective, it must be genuine. It is this sensitive and sincere "client-centeredness" in the therapeutic relationship that I regard as the third characteristic of nondirective therapy which sets it distinctively apart from other approaches.

SOME IMPLICATIONS

Although the client-centered approach had its origin purely within the limits of the psychological clinic, it is proving to have implications, often of a startling nature, for very diverse fields of effort. I should like to suggest a few of these present and potential implications.

In the field of psychotherapy itself, it leads to conclusions that seem distinctly heretical. It appears evident that training and practice in therapy should probably precede training in the field of diagnosis. Diagnostic knowledge and skill is not necessary for good therapy, a statement which sounds like blasphemy to many, and if the professional worker, whether psychiatrist, psychologist or caseworker, received training in therapy first he would learn psychological dynamics in a truly dynamic fashion, and would acquire a professional humility and willingness to learn from his client which is today all too rare.

The viewpoint appears to have implications for medicine. It has fascinated me to observe that when a prominent allergist began to use client-centered therapy for the treatment of non-specific allergies, he found not only very good therapeutic results, but the experience began to affect his whole medical practice. It has gradually meant the reorganization of his office procedure. He has given his nurses a new type of training in understanding the patient. He has decided to have all medical histories taken by a nonmedical person trained in nondirective techniques, in order to get a true picture of the client's feelings and attitudes toward himself and his health, uncluttered by the bias and diagnostic evaluation which is almost inevitable when a medical person takes the history and unintentionally distorts the material by his premature judgments. He has found these histories much more helpful to the physicians than those taken by physicians.

The client-centered viewpoint has already been shown to have significant implications for the field of survey interviewing and public opinion study. Use of such techniques by Likert, Lazarsfeld, and others has meant the elimination of much of the factor of bias in such studies.

This approach has also, we believe, deep implications for the handling of social and group conflicts, as I have pointed out in another paper. Our work in applying a client-centered viewpoint to group therapy situations, while still in its early stages, leads us to feel that a significant clue to the constructive solution of interpersonal and intercultural frictions in the group may be in our hands. Application of these procedures to staff groups, to inter-racial groups, to groups with personal problems and tensions, is under way.

In the field of education, too, the client-centered approach is finding significant application. The work of Cantor, a description of which will soon be published, is outstanding in this connection, but a number of teachers are finding that these methods, designed for therapy, produce a new type of educational process, an independent learning which is highly desirable, and even a reorientation of individual direction which is very similar to the results of individual or group therapy.

Even in the realm of our philosophical orientation, the client-centered approach has its deep implications. I should like to indicate this by quoting briefly from a previous paper.

As we examine and try to evaluate our clinical experience with client-centered therapy, the phenomenon of the reorganization of attitudes and the redirection of behavior by the individual assumes greater and greater importance. This phenomenon seems to find inadequate explanation in terms of the determinism which is the predominant philosophical background of most psychological work. The capacity of the individual to reorganize his attitudes and behavior in ways not determined by external factors nor by previous elements in his own experience, but determined by his own insight into those factors, is an impressive capacity. It involves a basic spontaneity which we have been loathe to admit into our scientific thinking.

The clinical experience could be summarized by saying that the behavior of the human organism may be determined by the influences to which it has been exposed, but it may also be determined by the creative and integrative insight of the organism itself. This ability of the person to discover new meaning in the forces which impinge upon him and in the past experiences which have been controlling him, and the ability to alter consciously his behavior in the light of this new meaning, has a profound significance for our thinking which has not been fully realized. We need to revise the philosophical basis of our work to a point where it can admit that forces exist within the individual which can exercise a spontaneous and significant influence upon behavior which is not predictable through knowledge of prior influences and conditionings. The forces released through a catalytic process of therapy are not adequately accounted for by a knowledge of the individual's previous conditionings, but only if we grant the presence of a spontaneous force within the organism which has the capacity of integration and redirection. This capacity for volitional control is a force which we must take into account in any psychological equation. So we find an approach which began merely as a way of dealing with problems of human maladjustment forcing us into a revaluation of our basic philosophical concepts.

SUMMARY

I hope that throughout this paper I have managed to convey what is my own conviction, that what we now know or think we know about a client-centered approach is only a beginning, only the opening of a door beyond which we are beginning to see some very challenging roads, some fields rich with opportunity. It is the facts of our clinical and research experience which keep pointing forward into new and exciting possibilities. Yet whatever the future may hold, it appears already clear that we are dealing with materials of a new and significant nature, which demand the most open-minded and thorough exploration. If our present formulations of those facts are correct, then we would say that some important elements already stand out; that certain basic attitudes and skills can create a psychological atmosphere which releases, frees, and utilizes deep strengths in the client; that these strengths and capacities are more sensitive and more rugged than hitherto supposed; and that they are released in an orderly and predictable process which may prove as significant a basic fact in social science as some of the laws and predictable processes in the physical sciences.

SELECTED REFERENCES

1. ALEXANDER, F. AND FRENCH, T. Psychoanalytic Therapy. New York: Ronald Press, 1946.

2. ALLEN, F. Psychotherapy with Children. New York: Norton, 1942.

3. CANTOR, N. Employee Counseling. New York: McGraw-Hill Book Company.

4. CANTOR, N. The Dynamics of Learning. (unpublished mss.) University of Buffalo, 1943.

5. CURRAN, C. A. Personality Factors in Counseling. New York: Grune and Stratton, 1945.

6. RANK, O. Will Therapy. New York: Alfred A. Knopf 1936.

7. ROGERS, C. R. "Counseling", Review of Educational Research. April 1945 (Vol. 15), pp. 135-163.

8. ROGERS, C. R. Counseling and Psychotherapy. New York: Houghton Mifflin Co., 1942.

9. ROGERS, C`. R. The implications of nondirective therapy for the handling of social conflicts. Paper given to a seminar of the Bureau of Intercultural Education, New York City, Feb. 18, 1946.

10. ROGERS. C. R. AND WALLEN, J. L. Counseling with Returned Servicemen. New York: McGraw-Hill, 1946.

11. SNYDER, W. "An Investigation of the Nature of Non-Directive Psychotherapy." Journal of Gen Psych. Vol. 33, 1945. pp.193-223.

12. TAFT, J. The Dynamics of Therapy in a Controlled Relationship. New York: Macmillan, 1933.

2. THE PROBLEM OF PSYCHOTHERAPY

(Laurance Shaffer 1947)

Originally presented as the address of the President of the Division of Clinical and Abnormal Psychology, American Psychological Association; this landmark paper draws attention to issues relating to the nature of the therapeutic process within psychotherapy which are just as relevant today:

How can we understand what takes place in the therapeutic interview? Why does it readjust the distressed person? Under what conditions is psychotherapy applicable? What techniques, applied in appropriately selected circumstances will produce predictable and effective results?

Shaffer's central argument is that the psychologist's major problem with respect to therapy is not that of the professional conditions of practice, but is the problem of understanding what therapy is and does.

Among all the interests of clinical psychologists, one stands pre-eminent in 1947 the interest in psychotherapy. This present concern with psychotherapy does not arise because it is a new activity for psychologists, as some persons outside of the profession have assumed. Remedial work with persons was one of the original functions of the first psychological clinic when it was founded half a century ago, and through all of the years since that time, some psychologists have been engaged in therapeutic work, not only in the educational sphere, but also in the broader areas designated as social, emotional, and personal. The phenomenon today is not that some psychologists are doing therapy, but that much greater numbers of them are doing it. Opportunities to serve human welfare have increased greatly, because of the recognition by local and national agencies, and by other professions, of the role of the psychologist as a therapist.

As with all human events, the causes of the enhanced interest in

21

therapy are complex and not a little obscure. In part, it is a symptom of a broad movement involving many professions that serve human interests. Psychiatry is experiencing the same revolution. We tend to think of all psychiatrists as therapists, but this has not always been so. Until quite recently, most psychiatrists were skilled primarily in diagnosis and institutional care, but now the dominant group in psychiatry has psychotherapy as its main interest. Social work and psychiatric nursing are also turning in this direction. In business and industry, personnel specialists are no longer occupied with selection and training alone but are interested in the total adjustments of workers as human beings. World War II brought all these professions together more intimately than in civilian life, and the resulting cross-fertilization has contributed markedly to the resultant flowering of the therapeutic attitude.

Psychologists have also turned to psychotherapy because of a growing dissatisfaction with their previous major function as mental testers. Even while the field of psychological measurement has become more complex and more entrancing, as tests have become more detailed, more diagnostic and more projective, it has remained unsatisfying for one reason alone. It does not cure. Psychologists are not satisfied with an adjunctive role, but want to get to the core of human betterment. Only psychotherapy offers this opportunity. Indeed, the contemporary reaction against testing may be going much too far, and it may be necessary to renew the emphasis on the positive values of objective psychological diagnosis.

A third reason for the growth of interest in therapy is the development of research techniques in this area. Research in therapy has had a circular effect. Originating from zeal, it has caused publication and discussion, has gained the respect of psychologists, and has therefore created ever widening circles of interest.

The spread of psychotherapy has given satisfactions but it has also brought problems. Questions have been raised as to who should be permitted to practice psychotherapeutic counseling. Should it be limited to psychiatrists; to the medical profession? Should legal certification or licensure be required of all who will engage in this practice so intimately bound to human welfare? How shall we train in the techniques of therapy the large numbers of students in clinical psychology that now flock to our universities and internship centers? Are the ethics of psychologists, until recently the academic ethics of scientists, sufficient for the more public responsibility that therapy implies? These questions show that the issue of psychotherapy has done much to precipitate the current professional problems of psychology, to which Committees and Boards of the American Psychological Association have devoted great attention during the past two years - problems of interprofessional relationships, of certification, of professional training and of ethics.

Important as these questions are, there is a more vital problem to be faced. This is the problem of the nature of the therapeutic process. How can we understand what takes place in the therapeutic interview? Why does it readjust the; distressed person? Under what conditions is psychotherapy applicable? What techniques, applied in appropriately selected circumstances will produce predictable and effective results? The psychologist's major problem with respect to therapy is not that of the professional conditions of practice, but is the problem of understanding what therapy is and does. In short, we need an explanation of therapy that will point the way to testable hypotheses concerning its nature and its improvement.

The word explanation is a dangerous one. It must be recognized that there is no such thing as a final and single explanation of any natural phenomenon. Every explanation must explain something to a certain audience of persons and for a certain purpose. An explanation of life insurance, for example, that would be satisfactory if addressed to a group of salesmen for the purpose of making them able to sell more insurance might be quite unsatisfying if addressed to actuaries whose purpose would be to compute the appropriate premium rates for a type of policy. Still another explanation would serve to make a customer want to buy.

Psychology furnishes many examples of explanations that serve various audiences and purposes. William James' (4) classic chapter on "Habit" is still charming reading, and may serve to inform and edify the intelligent layman who would obtain no sense of explanation at all from the volumes by Hull (3), Skinner (18) or Tolman (19) on essentially the same topic. An explanation of learning that is serviceable to a fifth grade teacher who wants to improve the arithmetic performance of her forty children would not be useful for a research specialist.

Explanations of psychotherapy may well be examined in the light of their purposes. A suitable initial illustration may be found in an early psychoanalytic explanation, first propounded but later denied by Freud. This example is appropriate because it shows the potential usefulness of an explanation, even though it may not be "true" (whatever that may mean). It can be cited without arousing defensive attitudes from any "school" of psychotherapy, since it has been discarded by its originator. This primitive Freudian theory held that psychotherapy is a process of catharsis, and that the patient is aided by getting him to recall forgotten memories of painful, emotionally toned experiences. The recollection of these memories was accompanied by a discharge of pent-up emotion, which came to be known as abreaction. Thus, the explanation advanced to account for the effect of psychotherapy was that it got this noxious, painful stuff out of the mind, from whence it issued with a loud explosion.

Was the theory of catharsis and abreaction a meaningless "explanation"? Not at all. It was a serviceable training device in the early days of psychoanalysis. Most significantly, it taught the early therapist that his client had to talk, preferably about painful experiences. It also prepared him for the client's emotional outbursts by indicating that they were a predictable part of the process of therapy then being used. Being forewarned, the therapist himself was not upset by the outburst of abreaction. A man unprepared for abreaction would have been alarmed by this turn of events, and might have taken flight into dermatology, or the study of visual configurations, or some other safer specialty, in order to preserve his own psychological balance! Far from being all "wrong," this discarded doctrine had a purpose when directed to an appropriate audience.

A similar function is served by certain aspects of later psychoanalytic theory. The concept of resistances gave the therapeutic worker patience in dealing with what common sense would have regarded as the stubbornness and uncooperativeness of his client. The theory of transference enabled him to regard calmly and dispassionately the emotional attachment, and the phases of emotional rejection that are induced by the psychoanalytic techniques of treatment. The concepts of resistance and transference serve as psychotherapy for the therapist himself. They make him feel secure against the surprises and conflicts of his task and protect him from feeling guilty about the disturbances he produces in the client.

A recent addition to the family of explanations of psychotherapy has been made by Rogers (14), in his nondirective approach. Like most psychotherapies, the nondirective methods seem first to have evolved gradually as a practice and only subsequently to have received a theoretical foundation. Nondirective therapy, however, has lately reached the degree of maturity indicated by the evolution of a theory. A basic concept has been stated by Rogers, ". . . within the client reside constructive forces whose strength and uniformity have been either entirely unrecognized or grossly underestimated. . .in most if not all individuals there exist growth forces, tendencies toward self-actualization, which may act as the sole motivation for therapy. . .The individual has the capacity and the strength to devise, quite unguided, the steps which will lead him to a more mature and more comfortable relationship to his reality. . . All of these capacities . . .

are released in the individual if a suitable psychological atmosphere is provided." (15, p. 418) This is an admirable explanation indeed, and nicely suited to its purpose. It persuades, even inspires, the nondirective counselor to refrain from coercion, advice, suggestion, and interpretation. Only a deep belief in the inner growth powers of the individual will keep the counselor in his nondirective role, supplying only the "atmosphere" of warmth, acceptance, and clarification. The theory is therefore an instructional method of great value, provided that the techniques that it inculcates are indeed effective ones.

This brief survey of some explanations of therapy shows that they operate principally on the level of action. These theories are methods of persuasion and methods of training. They are addressed to the audience of practicing therapists, and evoke the acceptance of the particular method that the theory commends. Furthermore, these theories have a personal value to the therapist that holds them. They give him a sense of security and protect him from conflicts of his own that might arise in the often uncomfortable interpersonal relationships of the therapeutic interview. Perhaps this last factor explains the warm, emotional, almost religious, attachment that each therapist has for his particular mode of explanation. The practicing therapist sees his theory not as an objective system of description, but as a code of values and a way of life.

An explanation that satisfies one purpose is often unstated for other purposes. It is not surprising, therefore, that theories inspired by needs for indoctrination and instruction are not completely satisfactory for another need - that for research, discovery, and development. Up to the present time, theories of psychotherapy have made relatively few contributions to research. The psychoanalytic theories have Indeed stimulated some research studies of high quality, such as those of Miller (8) on conflict and Mowrer (12) on regression, but these experimenters have drawn more from the hypotheses of the general psychology of learning than from clinical sources. The studies of Masserman (6) with cats most nearly fulfill the criteria of constructive research based on psychoanalytic hypotheses, but the findings have not yet been applied to the improvement of the processes of actual therapy. The meager results found by Scars (16) in his painstaking survey of objective studies of psychoanalytic concepts illustrate the shortcomings of this point of view as a guide to discovery. Practical improvements in psychoanalytic technique have arisen from experience rather than from the interactions of hypotheses and experimental studies, as is demonstrated in the recent book by Alexander and French (1).

Psychologists associated with Rogers' nondirective approach have made some excellent research studies. The current wave of interest in psychotherapy is due in large part to the favorable response to these researches. Even here, however, the connection between the basic theories of the school and the experimental design of their studies seems somewhat vague. The experiments have not yet attempted to verify or disprove hypotheses deduced from the fundamental postulates of the theory, although some current studies are beginning to approach this objective.

It may be concluded that psychotherapy's great need for a substantial scientific basis is not fulfilled with entire adequacy by any of the existing systematic approaches. Despite the claims of the conflicting schools, the effectiveness of psychotherapy leaves much to be desired. At the best, it probably gives significant help to only forty to sixty per cent of the clients who are subjected to its procedures. Even this degree of curative power is not well defined because of the absence of quantitative measurements of the severity of disturbance present at the outset, and of the exact extent of improvement achieved at the end of the counseling experience. The need to improve our psychotherapy is so great that ultimate gain probably would accrue if all psychologists stopped the practice of therapeutic counseling for the next few years and devoted their entire energies to research designed to increase the value of the process.

Several directions for research might be proposed. One obvious approach is the comparative evaluation of techniques now in use. We do not know, for example, the relative effectiveness of brief psychoanalysis a la Alexander, in comparison to nondirective counseling a la Rogers. Such comparisons of whole methods will probably be made, and may contribute by-products of permanent value, '('here is grave doubt, however, as to whether this is the most profitable orientation for research. First, the proponents of the various schools will have difficulty in agreeing on criteria of initial condition and of improvement. Second, existing whole theories are so emotionally toned and are so charged with personal value for their adherents that it is doubtful that anyone will be convinced. If there is anything that we know as clinical psychologists, it is the futility of attempting to resolve an emotional bias by intellectual argument. A third consideration is even more important. All entire methods, such as psychoanalysis and nondirective counseling, are complex. They have some elements in common and also differ in more than one respect. Experimental comparisons would therefore result either in a stalemate or in the partial vindication of one side or the other. Researches of this type would not be very likely to lead to new discoveries, to the detection of the particular excellences and faults of the methods, or to the synthesis of a new technique superior to all of its ancestors.

If existing theories are not suitable bases for research, an alternative must be sought to embark psychotherapy on its necessary voyage of discovery. A more profitable basis for the development of research might be the invention of new structures of theory. Such an attempt would start from a number of postulates and definitions, originating from observations and common points of agreement. From these postulates, testable hypotheses would then be proposed that might, lead to the design of experiments. These hypotheses would indicate the direction of a series of research studies, perhaps starting with animal experiments, and with experiments on segments of human behavior that can be controlled and quantified. Eventually, promising developments would be tried in actual therapy, if the evidence suggests a high probability of benefit, and a low probability of harm, to the experimental clients.

The advantages of such an approach are numerous. The experimenter in psychotherapy would be freed from personal attachment to a preconceived frame of reference. His identification with his brain-child would be the weaker one of the scientist for his idea rather than the stronger bias of the practical worker for a system of concepts on which his security depends. Therefore, he would be more able to follow the experimental evidence to its conclusions, to discard without undue pain an hypothesis that is unrewarding, and to invent new ones that seem to encompass a larger sphere of observations.

Some attempts to define the postulates of psychotherapy in terms suitable for research have already been made. For example, the research and theoretical articles of Mowrer (9, 10,11, 12, 13) have applied stimulus-response concepts to the study of adjustment mechanisms. The recent paper by Shaw (17) has extended this point of view to an explanation of some aspects of psychotherapy.

No single approach or unitary set of hypotheses is sufficient to attack the problem of psychotherapy, however, at our present stage of development. A dozen makers of theories are needed, each applying his hypotheses to experimental studies that will discover increasing numbers of relationships between observations. There is little danger that such a step would result in a number of warring little schools of thought, increasing the schism among psychologists. Instead, an anticipated outcome may be the elimination of dogmatic schools, as research findings take the place of contentions.

Of course, not all hypothetical structures are equally suitable for the advancement of psychotherapy through research. Some of the more obvious criteria for evaluating a theory may be suggested. First, the hypotheses should be in harmony with careful observations of the process. At least, no pertinent data concerning psychotherapy should be irreconcilably disharmonious with the theory. If a proposed theory cannot comprehend a commonly agreed observation, either the theory must be changed or the observation questioned. Second, the hypothesis should not have an immediate explanation for every aspect of psychotherapy. At first glance, this seems contradictory to the first premise. But a theory that reveals an area of frank ignorance is more likely to lead to an adventure of discovery than is one that smugly seems to account for all of the data. In fact, we are ignorant of many things about psychotherapy and an exposure of our gaps and shortcomings will be a primary objective of research. One of the faults of existing theories is that they claim to account for everything.

The third and most important requirement of a useful theory is that it must lead to the formulation of hypotheses for investigation that can be stated in testable terms and that lead to the design of experiments. As an illustration of the type of hypotheses that may serve as a basis for research, a partial theory of psychotherapy will be presented. This theory is proposed with a sense of humility. It is not intended to attract adherents or to found another school. Its value as a basis for indoctrination, inspiration, and instruction is probably low. On the other hand, it coordinates several things that we know about psychotherapy and points to an area of ignorance that challenges investigation.

A TENTATIVE HYPOTHESIS FOR PSYCHOTHERAPY

An approach to research in psychotherapy might start with a simple observational definition of what occurs in the therapeutic interview. Counseling is a conversation between persons. Essentially, they communicate, mainly by the use of words, although other media of communication, including acting out (as in play therapy and psychodrama), gesture, facial expression, and tone of voice are also present. Whatever other responses occur in the therapeutic situation are evoked by these words or word-substitutes, and are functionally related to them. Movements, tensions, visceral and glandular changes, attitudes, postures, images, and sub vocal verbalizations are among the secondary responses evoked by the interchange of words. This operational definition of the psychotherapeutic process in terms of observed happenings immediately suggests an investigation of the function of language in human adjustments.

There are many ways to study the operations of language. The analysis of the meanings of words in terms of semantics will be left, quite willingly, to others. There is also a behavioral approach to the functions of language. Talk may be used expressively, as when you say, "Ouch!" at the prick of a pin, or may give information, as when you say, "It is eight o'clock," although this apparently simplest use rarely occurs without some tinge of other functions. More importantly, language is used to control the behavior of others, in the guise of statements, requests, suggestions, and commands. Last, and here the enumeration reaches our present goal, language is used to control one's own behavior. This by no means novel concept suggests some relatively new hypotheses for an examination of psychotherapy.

In first condensed form, these hypotheses may be stated as follows:

1. An outstanding characteristic of the neurotic or maladjusted person is his inability to control his own behavior.

2. Normal persons control their behavior by the use of language signals, including the sub vocal and the gestural.

3. It follows that psychotherapy can be approached as a learning process through which a person acquires an ability to speak to himself in appropriate ways so as to control his own conduct.

The objection might be raised that these hypotheses are not dynamic, that they do not take into account the importance of motivation in cause and effect relationships. The concept of a neurotic lacking voluntary control may even seem to have an antique and moralistic ring. You associate it with futile admonitions about lacking "will power." On the contrary, no neglect of the motivational basis of human conduct is implied. Normal and neurotic behavior are alike in being motivated. The proposition that persons are striving organisms, that their behavior is determined by the satisfaction of needs and the avoidance of annoying stimulation, arose from psychopathology but has been extended to include normal people as well. The striving or dynamic character of persons is a similarity between the normal and the neurotic. We are looking for differences.

In pursuing the implications of these hypotheses, a first step might be an examination of the voluntary control of behavior by normal persons. The subject has been neglected by psychology, possibly because it is entangled in the philosophical difficulties of "free will." Due to the paucity of previous work, voluntary behavior is a frontier of normal psychology, ripe for an approach by research methods.

It seems probable that most of normal human behavior is mediated through self-signaling processes. If you have a letter in your hand and see a mail box, I he external object, the mail box itself, does not stimulate the appropriate behavior automatically, even though you have learned how to use post boxes in this total context. Instead, the visual perception of the mail box arouses vocal, sub vocal, gestural or sub gestural responses, which in turn evoke the appropriate motor behavior. This is a psychological description of what happens when you mail a letter "voluntarily."

If an element of discrimination, choice, or conflict is involved in the situation, the self-signaling becomes even more important. You may recall, that is, tell yourself, that there are no more mail collections today. Then you represent by a word or gesture the location of the post office several blocks down the street. At this moment, you have stimuli present to permit a discrimination response. You discriminate or choose, and either place the letter in the box or walk to the post office. The discrimination response is made possible by the presence of other verbal or near-verbal cues, relating to the importance of the prompt dispatch of the letter, the competition of the time required to walk to the post office with other activities, and other pertinent determiners. As in laboratory experiments, the discriminative response is facilitated by the presence of a wealth of cues to distinguish the choices.

One function of verbalization in a discrimination or conflict situation, then, is to bring the necessary cues into the present. Mowrer and Ullman (13) emphasized this point in discussing their experiment on the time factor in integrative learning. No one can discriminate between a past stimulus and a present one. Voluntary behavior is a choice reaction among immediate stimuli, some or all of which are verbal.

Our knowledge of how voluntary behavior is learned by normal persons is limited. Descriptive studies of children have suggested that a child learns to do an act in response to his own verbal stimulation by first learning to do it when told by others. Little children often give their self-instruction aloud, so that the process can be detected readily. Adult self-signaling is done by silent implicit speech, or by even more abbreviated postural and gestural stimuli. There is some clinical evidence that the reinforcement of self-signaling requires a dependency trustful relationship between a child and his parent, who supplies rewards for self-con I rolled behavior. In normal development, verbally-stimulated responses are reinforced more strongly and more frequently than are other types of reactions, so that voluntary control is learned.

There is also a modest amount of experimental evidence on the acquisition of voluntary control. Examples are the experiments of Menzies (7) on the conditioning of the voluntary control of an autonomic response, and of Davis (2) on the role of muscular tensions in thinking. On the whole, however, we are all too ignorant of how normal people acquire the important ability to regulate their conduct by means of their own signals.

An outstanding characteristic of maladjusted and neurotic persons is their inability to control their own behavior. We can picture some phobic person avoiding the mail box even when he "wants" to mail a letter; a sufferer from obsessive indecision pacing back and forth unable to decide between the box and the post office; a compulsive making sure that he has slammed the lid of the box exactly seven times, no more, no less. The neurotic's lack of self-control is also seen in more realistic clinical pictures: in anxiety neuroses, hysterias, so-called nervousness, phobias, and compulsions, and even in the ordinary defense mechanisms of compensation, rationalization, and the like.

Of course, the neurotic is not unable to respond to some kinds of inner signals. On the contrary, his anxiety is probably stimulated by visceral and proprioceptive cues. If a man has a phobia for cats, it is less the objective cat that induces his anxiety, than it is an inner pattern of tensions. Control, then, does not depend on the presence or absence of self-stimulation, but on the character of the stimuli and on the discriminative response that is made to them.

The psychoneurotic's lack of self-control has been recognized in the past, but it has been described in rather vague terms that have not encouraged experimental investigation. The most common statement, so widely used that its origin escapes detection, holds that the psychoneurotic lacks integration or wholeness of behavior. A recent variant is Lecky's (5) theory that the maladjusted personality does not have self-consistency. The psychic energy theories, based on the observed weakness and futility of psychoneurotic behavior, state that the ego lacks the strength required for dealing with reality. These theories have some explanatory value. Like all scientific generalizations, they are short formulas that draw together certain observed data. But they are lacking in another requisite of scientific hypotheses, in that they do not point the way to discovery. How shall we improve integration, or self-consistency, or ego-strength? More specific hypotheses are needed.

In terms of the hypotheses based on the functions of language in self-control, two characteristics of neurotic behavior may be distinguished. First, the neurotic does not respond with language to one or more significant aspects of his total situation. He represses, or shows resistance to the verbal representation of his problems, because recall is painful or conflict-producing. His inhibition of verbal responses has partial adjustive value. But, it prevents him from having available the cues on which to base a discriminative, voluntary, or normal response. This aspect of neurotic behavior is well recognized.

Second, the maladjusted person lacks control because the voluntary responses have not been reinforced with respect to the self-signal. It is common observation that the neurotic often "knows what he ought to do," but feels that he "is unable to do it." Something has prevented the establishment of connections between his own words and thoughts and his effective behavior.

The purposes of psychotherapy now become clear. They are, first, to induce the client to represent verbally the cues that he needs for normal voluntary behavior, and second, to reinforce appropriate responses to these verbal cues.

Existing systems of psychotherapy have been most successful in meeting the first requirement. Psychoanalytic therapy uses relaxation, free association, association with dreams, interpretation, the establishment of transference, and other techniques, to overcome resistances and encourage verbalization. Nondirective counseling has found that simple acceptance, evidence of warm interest, and reflection and clarification of feelings are serviceable for the same purposes. All of these techniques induce the verbalization of previously inhibited material. In many instances, they lead to "insight," a concept that is often regarded mystically, but that can be defined operationally as a verbalization of the person's problems and of the relationships between them. Although present methods are reasonably satisfactory for bringing about verbalization and insight, improvements might be sought. Further research may isolate the elements of these techniques, and vary them systematically so that the most effective composite is discovered. A method for inducing a client to talk must be judged not only by the ease with which it leads to verbalization, but also by its effect on the rest of the therapeutic process.

Insufficient attention has been paid to the second main requirement of psychotherapy, that of reinforcing responses to the client's own verbal cues. We have learned the first step of wisdom in recognizing that the stimuli to voluntary behavior must be the client's own, and not the therapist's. If you use suggestion or advice to solve a client's problems you are teaching him to respond to, and to depend on, your words rather than his words. The result may be the quick solution of one problem, but at the cost of establishing a dependence that will bring him running back to you when the next conflict arises.

Among current therapies, that of Rogers' holds that independence, planning, and voluntary behavior will arise spontaneously following the expressive features of the counseling. The counselor has only to provide the permissive "atmosphere" and the client's "growth" will take place. Unfortunately, "atmosphere" and "growth" are non-experimental terms in this context. It is probable that the permissive and non-punishing techniques of nondirective therapy do help some clients learn to make responses to their own words. If so, this is an incidental outcome, which rational therapy should regard as an intentional and major aim.

Psychoanalysis long has recognized something akin to the development of voluntary behavior. Freud himself wrote that the aim of therapy was ". . . to uncover repressions and replace them by acts of judgment. . ." Translating psychoanalytic practice into psychological concepts, the establishment and working through of transference might be regarded as a process of making the client repeat those stages of childhood that normally result in the acquisition of voluntary behavior. Just as a child acquires voluntary action through his dependence on a parent and through the rewards given by parents, so the person being psychoanalyzed might learn slowly through his relation to the analyst as a substitute parent image.

The repetition of the steps of childhood may not be the most efficient method for acquiring voluntary behavior, however. Indeed, it may be a very ineffective one. If you are helping an adult to overcome a speech defect, you do not try to regress him to a speechless infantile level and then retrain his speech from the beginning. This is not merely inefficient; it is quite impossible. An adult who lacks self-control must learn as an adult, and can hardly profit by a return to childishness.

The analysis of psychotherapy as a learning process involving the control of behavior by language signals has now reached its objective. The proposed hypotheses have uncovered an area of ignorance - we do not know enough about how people can learn to control their conduct by self-stimulating linguistic cues. This area is clearly susceptible to research. We can start with laboratory animals, by studying choice reactions based on intrabodily stimuli. A number of pertinent experiments already have been done, but few of them have been applied to concepts of therapy. We can move on to laboratory studies of human behavior, to test hypotheses concerning the influence of language on discrimination learning. The outcome should be some promising hypotheses for the final stage of clinical evaluation in actual therapy.

A theoretical structure is of value when it leads to specific and testable hypotheses for research. Let us explore the possibilities of a theory based on the concept of the learning of voluntary behavior.

An example of a particular hypothesis might be the following: The dependence of the client (or learner) upon the therapist (or teacher) is a condition favorable to the establishment of voluntary behavior. This may be stated as a null hypothesis for experimental evaluation: In learning responses to self-initiated stimuli, there is no significant difference between the conditions under which the learner is, or is not, dependent upon another human being who sets the rewards and punishments. Investigation of this hypothesis might clarify some of the differences between psychoanalytic therapy, with its emphasis on dependence, and nondirective therapy with its opposite assumptions.

Many other hypotheses suggest themselves. For example, you might investigate whether the learning of voluntary responses is facilitated when the cues are initiated by the learner, rather than when they are imposed by an external person, the teacher or therapist. This hypothesis leads readily to many experimental designs, ranging from rats in a Skinner (18) box, to actual therapeutic situations involving human subjects.

The theory that psychotherapy is a function of language does not offer a panacea. It is only one of an indefinite number of conceptual frameworks that might reveal areas for research. Others are needed. Approaches beginning with the concept of conflict, with the nature of anxiety, with the production and reduction of muscular tensions, and with other experimental hypotheses, will contribute to the advancement of our knowledge.

The major problem of psychotherapy today is its improvement through research. Schools and doctrines, conceived primarily to persuade and to teach, are unlikely to supply us with the basis for this improvement. The formulation of new hypotheses designed specifically to clarify issues and to lead to experiments, will guide us on the road to discovery. Only by understanding therapy, as well as by practicing therapy, can clinical psychology meet its new opportunities and its new obligations to serve human welfare.

REFERENCES

1. ALEXANDER, F., FRENCH, T. M. et al. Psychoanalytic therapy. New York: Ronald, 1946.

2. DAVIS, R. C. The relation of muscle action potentials to difficulty and frustration. J. exper. Psychol., 1938, 23, 141-158.

3. HULL, C. L. Principles of behavior. New York: Appleton-Century, 1943.

4. JAMES, W. Principles of psychology. New York: Holt, 1890.

5. LECKY, P. Self-consistency; a theory of personality. New York: Island Press, 1945.

6. MASSERMAN, J. H. Behavior and neurosis. Chicago: Univ. of Chicago Press, 1943.

7. MENZIES, R. Conditioned vasomotor responses in human subjects. J. Psychol, 1937, 4, 75-120.

8. MILLER, N. K. Experimental studies of conflict. In J. McV. Hunt (Kd.) Personality and the behavior disorders. New York: Ronald, 1944.

9. MOWRER, O. H. Frustration as an experimental problem. Some research implications of the frustration concept as related to social and educational problems. Character & Pers., 1938, 7, 129-135.

10. MOWRER, O. H. A stimulus response analysis of anxiety and its role as a reinforcing agent. Psychol. Rev., 1939, 46, 553-565.

11. MOWRER, O. H. Anxiety reduction and learning. J. exper. Psychol., 1940, 27, 497-516.

12. MOWRER, O. H. An experimental analogue of "regression" with incidental observations on "reaction formation." J. abnorm. soc. Psychol., 1940, 36, 56-87.

13. MOWRER, O. H. AND ULLMAN, A. D. Time as a determinant in integrative learning. Psychol, Rev., 1945, 52, 61-90.

14. ROGERS, C. R. Counseling and psychotherapy. Boston: Houghton Mifflin, 1942.

15. ROGERS, C. R. Significant aspects of client-centered therapy. Amer. Psychologist, 1946, 1, 415-422.

16. SEARS, R. R. Survey of objective studies of psychoanalytic concepts. New York: Social Science Research Council, 1943.

17. SHAW, F. J. A stimulus-response analysis of repression and insight in psychotherapy. Psychol. Rev., 1946, 53, 36-42.

18. SKINNER, B. F. The behavior of organisms. New York: Appleton-Century, 1938.

19. TOLMAN, E. C. Purposive behavior in animals and men. New York: Century, 1932.

3. PSYCHOTHERAPY AND THE PLACEBO EFFECT

(David Rosenthal & Jerome D. Frank 1956)

This classic article describes the placebo effect, discusses some of its implications for the evaluation of psychotherapy, and makes recommendations concerning research design in psychotherapy based on these considerations.

It is by now generally recognized that all forms of psychotherapy yield successful results with some patients and that these successes depend to an undetermined extent on factors common to many types of relationship between patient and therapist. This poses a knotty problem for proponents of various specific forms of psychotherapy who are convinced that their successes result from their particular theory or technique and wish to convince others of this. As a result, problems of research design in psychotherapy have been receiving more and more critical attention in recent years, especially with reference to controls (6, 11, 20, 23, 24, 25, 27, 31, 34, 35, 38, 39).

Certain general aspects of the psychotherapeutic relationship seem very similar to those responsible for the so-called placebo effect, which is well known to investigators of the therapeutic efficacy of medications. The purpose of this paper is to describe the placebo effect, discuss some of its implications for the evaluation of psychotherapy, and make some recommendations concerning research design in psychotherapy based on these considerations.

THE PLACEBO EFFECT

We have now participated in two separate investigations of the effectiveness of drugs on the symptomatic distress of psychiatric outpatients (14, 22). Both studies involved the administration of a placebo, an inert agent outwardly indistinguishable from the agent being tested, as well 294 as drugs. The physician never knew whether he was giving the patient drug or placebo. The patients were told that a new medicine had become available which, it was thought, might help them. The physicians rated symptoms on a 4- point scale of distress, with high reliability. In both studies a significant reduction of distress accompanied the taking of placebos.

This phenomenon occurs with great regularity, not only with respect to the kinds of symptoms usually associated with psychologic illness, but with others as well. For example, in a study of vaccines for the common cold, there was found a reduction in the number of yearly colds of 55 per cent among those given vaccine and of 61 per cent among a control group who received injections of isotonic sodium chloride solution (4). Hillis (15) found placebos as effective as other agents in inhibiting the cough reflex. Wolf and Pinsky (37) studied medical outpatients suffering from peptic ulcer, migraine, muscle tension, headache, and tight muscles in the extremities. All were also tense and anxious. Twenty to thirty per cent felt better while taking placebos. Lasagna et al. (19) gave 1 ml of saline by subcutaneous injection to surgical patients suffering from steady, severe wound pains and found that 30 to 40 per cent reported a satisfactory relief of pain. In a study by Jellinek (18) 60 per cent of 199 subjects with chronic headaches received relief from a placebo on one or more occasions.

The placebo effect is not always favorable, but may also result in undesirable, distressful reactions. As far back as 1933, Diehl (3) using lactose placebos as a control for a variety of medications taken by mouth, found that some of his subjects receiving placebos developed nausea, faintness, and diarrhea. Sometimes this "toxic response" to placebos may even attain major proportions. Wolf and Pinsky (37) tell of one patient who had "overwhelming weakness, palpitation, and nausea within 15 minutes of taking her tablets." In another, "a diffuse itchy erythematous maculopapular rash developed after ten days of taking pills. A skin consultant considered the eruption to be typical dermatitis medicamentosa. After use of the pills was stopped, the eruption quickly cleared." A third patient developed epigastric pain followed by watery diarrhea, urticaria, and angioneurotic edema of the lips within ten minutes of taking her pills. One of our own patients, who had been tolerating a chronic syphilophobia fairly well, became acutely agitated shortly after placebo ingestion, bemoaning what the pills had done to him, and required hospitalization shortly thereafter.

Wolf and Pinsky (37) found that placebos produced more improvement in subjective than objective manifestations of anxiety and tension, but objective changes also occur. In our second study (22), 69 per cent of our patients showed decreased blood pressure and pulse readings following placebo, 19 per cent showed increased blood pressure, and 25 per cent showed a rise in pulse rate. Wolf (36) demonstrated clearly and convincingly that actual end-organ changes can follow placebo administration. This demonstration was made in a series of studies on the now-celebrated Tom, a human subject with a large gastric fistula, in whom it was possible to observe directly the gastric mucous membrane, correlating changes in color and turgidity with simultaneous measurements of gastric secretion and motor activity.

The placebo effect may actually reverse the normal pharmacologic action of a drug. For example, Wolf reports that Tom was repeatedly given Prostigmine, which induced abdominal cramps, diarrhea, as well as hyperaemia, hypersecretion, and hypermotility of the stomach. Subsequently, the same response occurred not only to tap water and lactose capsules, but also to atropine sulfate which usually has an inhibiting effect on gastric function. A pregnant patient with excessive vomiting showed the usual response of nausea and vomiting to ipecac. These manifestations were accompanied by cessation of normal gastric contractions. When ipecac was given through a tube with strong assurance that it would relieve her vomiting, gastric contractions were resumed at the same interval after ingestion of the drug that they would normally have ceased, and her nausea and vomiting were relieved.

The placebo effect, in short, can be quite powerful. It can significantly modify the patient's physiological functioning, even to the extent of reversing the normal pharmacological action of drugs; and, as will be discussed below, it may be enduring. Placebo effects cannot be dismissed as superficial or transient. They often involve an increased sense of well-being in the patient and are manifested primarily by relief from the particular symptomatic distress for which the patient expects and receives treatment. Thus, the relief of any particular complaint by a given medication is not sufficient evidence for the specific effect of the medicine on this complaint unless it can be shown that the relief is not obtained as a placebo effect.

IMPLICATIONS OF THE PLACEBO EFFECT FOR RESEARCH IN PSYCHOTHERAPY

The giving of any medication may have certain meanings for a patient in terms of his relationship to his physician which may benefit his condition irrespective of the pharmacological action of the drug. For example, it may relieve the anxiety resulting from the distress caused by his illness (10), Wolf believes the effects of placebos on his patients "depended for their force on the conviction of the patient that this or that effect would result." The degree of the patient's conviction might be expected to be influenced by his previous experiences with doctors, his confidence in his physician, his suggestibility, the suggestibility-enhancing aspects of the situation in which the therapeutic agent is being administered, and his faith in or fear of the therapeutic agent itself. These attitudes are obviously relevant to psychotherapy. Psychotherapists have theories of personality and psychotherapy and plan their therapeutic actions in the belief that these are the active agents which produce the desired results. Any favorable changes in patients consequent to a course of psychotherapy tend to be cited as evidence for the validity of the theory of personality and neurosis which underlie the rationale of the psychotherapy. In view of the above discussion it may well be that the efficacy of any particular set of therapeutic operations lies in their analogy to a placebo in that they enhance the therapist's and patient's conviction that something useful is being done. Patients entering psychotherapy have various degrees of belief in its efficacy, and this may be an important factor in the results of therapy, but this has not been studied, to our knowledge. We know that the authoritarian attitude of the physician can produce this conviction in some patients.

At first glance the attitudes found by Fiedler (8, 9) to characterize experienced psychotherapists, viz. feelings of empathy for and closeness to the patient, an undemanding attitude, security, and the ability to "understand" the patient, seem diametrically opposed to the authoritarian attitude. It may be, however, that the therapeutic efficacy of these attitudes lies primarily in their ability to increase the confidence of certain patients in the ability of the therapist to help them. Lack of such confidence may be one of the reasons why patients of lower socioeconomic status fare less well in psychotherapy than patients higher in this scale (16, 29), a talking therapy seeming to be beyond their comprehension and contrary to their conception of the doctor-patient relationship.

In this connection, the role of suggestion in psychotherapy has been emphasized for years, especially in therapies utilizing hypnosis, but suggestion effects have been thought by many since Freud to be superficial and transitory. We know of no experimental study which demonstrates that therapeutic effects based on insights or perceptual reorganization, which may also be suggested, are less superficial or less transitory.

It may be pointed out parenthetically that conviction of the helpfulness of therapy need not be equated with "motivation for therapy," which was investigated by Grummon (13) and Dymond (5) and found to have little relationship to success in psychotherapy. Patients are often sufficiently distressed to be strongly motivated to receive help, yet have little faith that a procedure such as psychotherapy can help them.

The similarity of the forces operating in psychotherapy and the placebo effect may account for the high consistency of improvement, rates found with various therapies, from that conducted by physicians without psychiatric training to intensive psychoanalysis (7). This explanation gains plausibility from the fact that reported improvement rates for various series of neurotics treated by different forms of psychotherapy hover around 60 per cent (1). This is the same as that reported for the placebo effect in illnesses in which emotional components may play a major role such as "colds" (3) and headaches (18).

To show that a specific form of treatment produces more than a nonspecific placebo effect it must be shown that its effects are stronger, last longer, or are qualitatively different from those produced by the administration of placebos, or that it affects different types of patients. Our knowledge of all these matters is still fragmentary, but some beginnings have been made.

With respect to the strength and qualitative nature of the effects of therapy, one line of endeavor has been to study the physiological changes occurring during psychotherapy. Since physiological measures usually used to provide evidence of resistance or frustration (26, 33) or similar psychological states during psychotherapy (28) may also be influenced by the placebo effect, one cannot conclude that demonstration of such physiological changes implies a greater depth of therapy or a more profound reorganization of the personality, unless we are willing to equate the placebo effect with such reorganization.

With respect to the duration of improvement, if it could be shown that the placebo effect is of shorter duration than changes specific to a given psychotherapy, this would provide one kind of evidence favoring that theory of psychotherapy. As far as we know, no study of the limits of duration of the placebo effect has been made. Our experiment with mephenesin vs. placebo covered four two-week periods.

The greatest decrease in distress following placebos was felt during the first two-week trial period. After that, a slight but statistically insignificant rise in distress occurred; and, at the end of eight weeks, the placebo effect was about as great as after two weeks. Unfortunately, our data yielded no information on how much longer it might have endured. If the effect is analogous to the relief of pain by placebos in patients with surgical wounds, we should expect it eventually to diminish. Lasagna et al. (19) found that as placebo therapy of such patients continued the relief experienced decreased. Although the number of patients is too small to justify any conclusions, it is intriguing that the first dose of mephenesin seemed to counteract the placebo effect. In the study with reserpinc (22), the only patients who failed to show a placebo effect were those who had received reserpinc previously. It may be that any discomfort produced by a pharmacologically active agent tends to counteract the emotional state responsible for a placebo effect in susceptible patients. Analogously, an activity by the psychotherapist which disturbs the patient may conceivably counteract the placebo effect of psychotherapy with certain patients.

It would also be helpful to know if patients could be differentiated according to attributes which predisposed them to a positive or negative placebo effect. If patients who improved with a particular form of psychotherapy were all known to be positive placebo reactors, then the improvement could not be attributed to the specific form of treatment. If, however, they were known not to be positive placebo reactors, then any demonstrated improvement would constitute evidence of efficacy specific to the form of psychotherapy.

There is little known, however, with regard to the attributes of placebo reactors. Lasagna et al. (19) have made the first attempts to investigate this problem and report some attitudes and Rorschach categories which differentiated their reactors (N=11) from their nonreactors (N=16). However, only 14 per cent of their patients were consistent reactors, i.e., showed the effect with every placebo dose, and 31 per cent were consistent nonreactors, while 55 per cent showed the effect on some occasions but not on others. This contrasts with the findings of Jellinek (18) whose patients with headache were, for the most part, cither in the always-relieved group or the never-relieved group, with only a small percentage of patients showing inconsistency of response. The apparent contradiction in findings may perhaps result from the difference in the cause of the pain in the two series or from other factors. In any case it indicates that the problem is a complex one needing much more study. In the light of these considerations, any method of demonstrating the specificity of response to a given type of psychotherapy would have to provide an adequate control design. As far as we know, the study which has paid closest attention to the question of controls in research in psychotherapy is that of Rogers and his colleagues (31). They employed two different kinds of control groups. One was a group of non-clients who were simply given a battery of tests before and after specified time periods. The other was a group of clients who were required to wait a specified period of time before beginning therapy. This group was tested at the beginning and end of the wait period, at the end of therapy, and after a follow-up period.

These procedures do not control for the placebo effect since neither control group was being subjected to any special procedures which could produce a reasonable expectancy in control subjects that certain changes should occur. The experimental group, however, could be expected to anticipate certain effects merely as a consequence of participating in the client- therapist interviews. Therefore, even though favorable changes could be demonstrated in their clients, the question of whether these were placebo effects could not be answered from such research design unless additional information were provided.

If we do not control for nonspecific factors like the placebo effect, we cannot know whether effects predicted from a theory lead to or result from improvement based on the nonspecific effect. Butler and Haigh (2), for example, report an increased correlation of perceived self with ideal self following client-centered therapy. The implicit inference is that the specific therapeutic method leads to this increased correlation which, in turn, contributes to amelioration of disability and distress.

It is conceivable, though, that as a result of a nonspecific placebo effect the client feels less disabled and distressed which, in turn, leads him to describe himself as more like his ideal self. Rogers' (30) findings of greater emotional maturity in successfully treated cases may be similarly explained, clients feeling less disabled and distressed due to a nonspecific placebo response and behaving consequently in ways which are less anxiety-determined and which are seen as more mature by others.

We would propose that the following conditions are optimal in planning research in psychotherapy:
1. A theory of personality and psychological distress (neurosis,

maladjustment, etc.).

2. Predictions of effects in the patient or client consequent to psychotherapy, in accord with the theory.

3. Demonstration of a relationship between the predicted effects and some criterion of improvement.

4. Demonstration that the predicted effects and their relationship to the improvement criterion are not due primarily to the patient's conviction that therapy will help him. This will permit greater confidence that the relationship found is specific to the therapeutic technique derived from the theory.

Ideally, these conditions should obtain both for process and outcome research. There seems to be general agreement with regard to the first two conditions although Mackinnon (21) has some reservations about beginning with a theory rather than a hunch. Gordon et al. (12) have come to question the third condition, at least with respect to a "global" criterion of improvement.

The fourth condition has not been met in any research of which we are aware. It is not possible to set up an experiment precisely analogous to comparison of a medication with a placebo because there is no such thing as inert psychotherapy in the sense that placebos are pharmacologically inert. However, it may be possible to study the possible specific effects of any particular form of therapy by the use of a matched control group participating in an activity regarded as therapeutically inert from the standpoint of the theory of the therapy being studied. That is, it would not be expected to produce the effects predicted by the theory. The "placebo psychotherapy" in this sense would be analogous to placebos in that it would be administered under circumstances and by persons such that the patients would expect to be helped by it.

Let us say that our theory is psychoanalytic and our predicted effect is an increased correlation between the moral values of the patient and the therapist (superego identification) and that we also expect an association between the increased correlation and a criterion of improvement (32). According to the theory, there is no reason to believe that control patients receiving, for example, relaxation therapy (17) will show the increased correlation of moral values with their therapist's moral values, nor should they show as much or as lasting improvement as the patients receiving psychoanalytic therapy of equal length. Such a design would constitute a fair test of the hypothesis based on the theory. In comparative studies where one type of psychotherapy is tested against another, differences found between them in predicted effects or amount, nature, and duration of improvement would not be explainable as placebo effects, if the condition could be met that patients had equal faith in the efficacy of the therapies and therapists to which they are assigned.

SUMMARY AND CONCLUSIONS

The literature on the therapeutic efficacy of drugs compared with placebos is briefly reviewed, and its relevance for research in psychotherapy considered. It is concluded that improvement under a special form of psychotherapy cannot be taken as evidence for: (a) correctness of the theory on which it is based; or (b) efficacy of the specific technique used, unless improvement can be shown to be greater than or qualitatively different from that produced by the patients' faith in the efficacy of the therapist and his technique — "the placebo effect." This effect may be thought of as a nonspecific form of psychotherapy and it may be quite powerful in that it may produce endorgan changes and relief from distress of considerable duration.

REFERENCES

1. APPEL, K. E., LHAMON, W. T., MYERS, J. M., & HARVEY, W. A. Long term psychotherapy. In Psychiatric treatment. Proc. Ass. Res. Nerv. Ment. Dis. Dec. 14, IS, 1951, New York. Baltimore: Williams & Wilkins, 1953, 21-34. 2.

2.BUTLER, J. M., & HAIGH, G. V. Changes in the relation between self-concepts and ideal concepts consequent upon client-centered counseling. In C. R. Rogers & Rosalind F. Dyraond (Eds.), Psychotherapy and personality change, Chicago: Univer. of Chicago Press, 1954. Pp. 55-75.

3. DIEHL, II. S. Medical treatment of the common cold. J. Amer. Med. Ass., 1933, 101, 2042-2045.

4. DIEHL, H. S., BAKER, A. B., & COWAN, D. W. Cold vaccines, further evaluation. J. Amer. Med. Ass., 1940, 115, 593-594.

5. DYMOND, ROSALIND F. Adjustment changes in the absence of psychotherapy. J. consult. Psychol., 1955, 19, 103-107.

6. EDWARDS, A. L., & CRONBACII, L. J. Experimental design for research in psychotherapy. J. din. Psychol., 1952, 8, 51-59.

7. EYSENCK, H. J. The effects of psychotherapy — An evaluation. J. consult. Psychol., 1952, 16, 319-324.

8. FIEDLER, F. E. The concept of the ideal therapeutic relationship. J. consult. Psychol., 1950, 14, 239-245.

9. FIEDLER, F. E. A comparison of therapeutic relationships in psychoanalytic, nondirective, and Adlerian therapy. J. consult. Psychol, 1950, 14, 436-445.

10. FRANK, J. D. Psychotherapeutic aspects of symptomatic treatment. Amer. J. Psychiat., 1946, 103, 21-25.

11. GREENHILL, M. H., FORD, L. S., OLSON, W. C., RYAN, W. C., WHITMAN, S., & SKEELS, H. M. Evaluation in mental health, Bethescla: National Institute of Mental Health, 1955.

12. GORDON, T., GRUMMON, D. L., ROGERS, C. R., & SEEMAN, J, Developing a program of research in psychotherapy. In C. R. Rogers & Rosalind F. Dymond (Eds.) Psychotherapy and personality change. Chicago: Univer. of Chicago Press, 1954. Pp. 12-34.

13. GRUMMON, D. L. Personality changes as a function of time in persons motivated for therapy. In C. R. Rogers & Rosalind F. Dymond (Eds.), Psychotherapy and personality change. Chicago: Univer. of Chicago Press, 1954, 238-255.

14. HAMPSON, J. L., ROSENTHAL, D., & FRANK, J. D. A comparative study of the effects of mephenesin and placebo on the symptomatology of a mixed group of psychiatric outpatients. Bull. Johns Hopkins Hasp., 1954, QS, 170-177.

15. HILLIS, B. R. The assessment of cough-suppressing drugs. Lancet, 1952, 1, 1230-1232.

16. IMBER, S. D., NASH, E. H., & STONE, A. R. Social class and duration of psychotherapy. J. din. Psychol., in press.

17. JACOBSON, E. Progressive relaxation. Chicago: Univer. of Chicago Press, 1938.

18. JELLINEK, E. M. Clinical tests on comparative effectiveness of analgesic drugs. Biometrics Bull, 1946, 2, 87.

19. LASAGNA, L., MOSTELLER, F., FELSINGER, J. M., & BEECHER, H. K. A study of the placebo response. Amer. J. Med., 1954, 16, 770-779.

20. LEBO, D. The present status of research on nondirective play therapy. J. consult. Psychol, 1953, 17, 177-183.

21. MACKINNON, D. W. Fact and fancy in personality research. Amer. Psychol. 1953, 8, 138-145.

22. MEATH, J. A., FELDBERG, T. M., ROSENTHAL, D., & FRANK, J. D. A comparative study of reserpine and placebo in the treatment of psychiatric outpatients. (Unpublished manuscript.)

23. MORSE, P. W. A proposed technique for the evaluation of psychotherapy. Amer. J. Orthopsychiat., 1953, 4, 716-731.

24. MOSAK, H. H. Problems in the definition and measurement of success in psychotherapy. L. W. Wolff & J. A. Preckcr: Sitccess in psychotherapy. New York: Grime & Stratton, 1952, 1-25.

25. MOWRER, O. H. (Ed.). Psychotherapy: theory and research. New York: Ronald, 1953.

26. MOWRER, O. H., LIGHT, B. H., LURIZ, Z., & ZELENY, M. P. Tension changes during psychotherapy, with special reference to resistance. In O. H. Mowrer (Ed.) Psychotherapy: theory and research. New York: Ronald, 1953, Pp. 546-640.

27. OBERNDORF, C. P., GREENACRE, PHYLLIS, & KUBIE, L. Symposium on the evaluation of therapeutic results. Int. J. Psychoanal, 1948, 29, 7- 33.

28. O'KELLY, L. I. Physiological changes during psychotherapy. In

O. H. Mowrer (Ed.) Psychotherapy: theory and research. New York: Ronald 1953, 641-656.

29. REDLICH, F. C., HOLLINGSHEAD, A. B., ROBERTS, B. II., ROBINSON, H. A., FREEDMAN, L. Z., & MYERS, J. K. Social structure and psychiatric disorders. Amer. J. Psychiat., 1953, 109, 729-734.

30. ROGERS, C. R. Changes in the maturity of behavior as related to therapy. In C. R. Rogers & Rosalind F. Dymond (Eds.) Psychotherapy and personality change. Chicago: Univer. of Chicago Press, 1954. Pp. 215-237.

31. ROGERS, C. R., & DYMOND, ROSALIND F. (Eels.) Psychotherapy and personality change. Chicago: Univcr. of Chicago Press, 1954.

32. ROSENTHAL, D. Changes in some moral values following psychotherapy. J. consult. Psychol., 1955, 19, 431-436.

33. THETFORD, W. N. An objective measurement of frustration tolerance in evaluating psychotherapy. In W. Wolff & J. A. Precker, Success in psychotherapy. New York: Grime & Stratton, 1952, 26-62.

34. THORNE, F. C. Rules of evidence in the evaluation of the effects of psychotherapy. J. din. Psychol., 1952, 8, 38-41.

35. WATSON, R. I., MENSCH, I., & GILDEA, E. F. The evaluation of the effects of psychotherapy III. Research design. J. Psychol., 1951, 32, 293 -308.

36. WOLF, S. Effects of suggestion and conditioning on the action of chemical agents in human subjects—the pharmacology of placebos. J. din. Invest., 1950, 29, 100-109.

37. WOLF, S., & PINSKY, R. H. Effects of placebo administration and occurrence of toxic reactions. J. Amer. Med. Ass., 1954, 155, 339-341.

38. WOLFF, W., & PRECKER, J. A. Success in psychotherapy. New York: Grime & Stratton, 1952.

39. ZUBIN, J. Design for the evaluation of therapy. In Psychiatric treatment. Proc. Ass. Res. Nerv. Ment. Dis. Dec. 14, 15, 1951, New York. Baltimore: Williams & Wilkins, 1953. Pp. 10-15.

4. RATIONAL PSYCHOTHERAPY AND INDIVIDUAL PSYCHOLOGY

(Albert Ellis 1957)

This classic article was one of the first published accounts of rational psychotherapy; a theory of personality and a system of therapeutic technique that would eventually develop into what is now known as rational emotive behavior therapy.

In the course of this landmark paper Ellis introduces and expands upon his hypothesis that thinking represents the most important way in which human emotion is caused and controlled. He then goes on to outline the main points of agreement and disagreement between rational therapy and the individual Psychology of Alfred Adler.

Rational psychotherapy is a theory of personality and a system of therapeutic technique which has evolved from the writer's clinical practice over the last decade. Although, like all modern psychodynamic theorizing, it owes an inestimable debt to the thinking of Sigmund Freud (12, 13), it has philosophic roots in the rational analyses of some of the early philosophers, such as Epictetus (1), and psychological roots in the persuasive techniques of some of the late nineteenth century therapists, such as Dubois (5).

When the first public paper on rational psychotherapy was presented in 1956 (10), it was pointed out by Dr. Rudolf Dreikurs and others that there seemed to be a close connection between many of viewers expounded by the writer and some of the basic thinking of Alfred Adler. This connection will now be examined, to determine what are the main points of agreement and disagreement between rational therapy and individual Psychology.

RATIONAL PSYCHOTHERAPY

Rational psychotherapy starts with the hypothesis that human emotion is caused and controlled in several major ways and that, for all practical purposes, the most important of these is usually by thinking. Much of what we call emotion is nothing more or less than a certain kind - a biased, prejudiced, or strongly evaluative kind - of thought. Since, in our culture, thinking normally takes place in terms of language, positive human emotions, such as feelings of love or elation, generally result from conscious or unconscious sentences stated in some form or variation of the phrase "This is good!" and negative human emotions, such as feelings of anger or depression, generally are caused by some form or variation of the sentence "This is bad!" If an adult would not employ, on some conscious or unconscious level, such sentences, much of his emoting simply would not exist.

If human emotions largely result from thinking, then one may appreciably control one's feelings by controlling one's thoughts - or by changing the internalized sentences, or self-talk, with which one largely created the feeling in the first place. This is what the rational therapist teaches his clients to do: to understand exactly how they create their own emotional reactions by telling themselves certain things, and how they can create different emotional reactions by telling themselves other things.

The rational therapist believes that emotional disturbance essentially arises when individuals tell themselves negative, unrealistic, illogical, self-defeating sentences. He further believes that, for the most part, disturbed individuals are not aware that they are talking to themselves illogically; or of what the irrational links in their internalized sentences are; or of how they can learn to tell themselves saner and more realistic thoughts or sentences. This is the therapist's main task: to make them aware - or conscious - of their inner verbalizations.

Although it is possible that some of man's illogical ideas are rooted in his biological limitations, it seems clear that many or most of them are inculcated or over-emphasized by his upbringing, especially by (a) his parents, (b) his teachers, and (c) his contact with his general culture and particularly the media of mass communication in this culture. As a result of these biosocial conditions, virtually all humans in our society hold several major illogical ideas or philosophies which inevitably lead to some measure of self-defeat and neurosis.

Some of the most important irrational ideas which are presently ubiquitous in our culture are these: (1) the idea that it is a dire necessity for an adult human being to be loved or approved by everyone for everything he does; (2) the idea that one should be thoroughly competent, adequate, and achieving in all possible respects; (3) the idea that certain people are bad, wicked, or villainous, and that they should be severely punished and blamed for their villainy; (4) the idea that it is terrible, horrible, and catastrophic when things are not the way one would like them to be; (5) the idea that human unhappiness is externally caused, and people have little or no ability to control their sorrows and disturbances; (6) the idea that if something is, or may be dangerous or fearsome, one should be terribly concerned about it; (7) the idea that it is easier to avoid than to face certain life difficulties and self-responsibilities; (8) the idea that one should be dependent on others and needs someone stronger than oneself on whom to rely; (9) the idea that the past is all-important and that because something once strongly affected one's life, it should indefinitely have the same effect; (10) the idea that one should become quite upset over other people's problems and disturbances; (11) the idea that it is exceptionally difficult to find the right solution to many human problems, and that if the precise and correct solution is not found the results will be catastrophic; (12) the idea that human happiness can be achieved by inertia and inaction.

The rational therapist believes that ideas like these can be prove to be illogical, unworkable, and self-defeating (though, for lack of space, no attempt to prove this will be made in the present paper); and that when clients are forcefully disabused of these unrealistic beliefs they steadily, and often with remarkable speed, overcome their emotional disturbances. The therapist frequently employs the usual expressive-emotive, supportive, relationship, and insight-interpretive techniques which the present author (7, 8) has outlined elsewhere. But where most therapists directly or indirectly show the client that he is behaving illogically, the rational therapist goes beyond this point to make a forthright, unequivocal attack on the client's general and specific irrational ideas and to try to induce him to adopt more rational ones in their place.

Rational psychotherapy makes a concerted attack on the disturbed individual's irrational positions in two main ways: (a) the therapist serves as a frank counter-propagandist who directly contradicts and denies the self-defeating propaganda and superstitions which the client originally learned and keeps self-propagandistically perpetuating. (b) The therapist encourages, persuades, cajoles, and at times commands the client to partake of some kind of activity which itself will act as a forceful counter-propagandist agency against the nonsense he believes. Both these therapeutic acts are consciously performed with the goal of finally getting the client to internalize a rational philosophy of living just as he originally internalized the irrational ideas and attitudes of his parents and his culture.

SIMILARITIES WITH INDIVIDUAL PSYCHOLOGY

These, very sketchily expounded, are some of the central hypotheses of rational psychotherapy. Although they were evolved largely from empirical observation, and within the framework of a highly eclectic orientation, objective analysis will show that they significantly overlap at many points with the views of Alfred Adler, and that Adler unquestionably had priority in boldly expressing these views.

Rational therapy, for example, holds that it is people's irrational beliefs or attitudes which usually determine their significant emotions reactions and lead to their disturbances. Adler continually emphasized the importance of the individual's style of life (4, p. 2) and insisted that "The psychic life of man is determined by his goals' (1, p. 19). The common factor is that both, beliefs and attitudes, and goals, are a form of thought.

Adler noted that when an individual is neurotic, "We must decrease his feeling of inferiority by showing him that he really under values himself' (2, p. 112). Rational therapists teach their clients that their feelings of inadequacy invariably arise from the irrational beliefs that they should be thoroughly competent in everything they do, and that they should severely blame themselves when they make any mistakes or when someone disapproves of them.

The rational therapist makes relatively little use of the Freudian notion of a highly dramatic "unconscious" in which sleeping motivations lie ever ready to rise up and smight the individual with neurotic symptoms (6, 9), but he does keep showing his clients that they are unconsciously, or unwarily, telling themselves statements, naively believing these unconsciously-perpetuated statements, and significantly affecting their own conduct thereby. Adler says much the same thing in these words: "The unconscious is nothing other than that which we have been unable to formulate in clear concepts. It is not a matter of concepts hiding away in some unconscious or subconscious recesses of minds, but of parts of our consciousness, the significance which we have not fully understood" (4, pp. 232-233).

Adler points out that the therapist "must be so convinced of the uniqueness and exclusiveness of the neurotic direction line, that he is able to foretell the patient's disturbing devices and construction, always to find and explain them, until the patient, completely upset

61

gives them up - only to put new and better hidden ones in the place" (4, p. 334). This, in his own terms, is exactly what the rational therapist does, because he knows, even before he talks to the client that this client must believe some silly, irrational ideas - otherwise he could not possibly be disturbed. And, knowing this, the rational therapist deliberately looks for these irrationalities, often predicts them, and soon discovers and explains them, or mercilessly reveals their flaws, so that the client is eventually forced to give them up and replace them with more rational philosophies of living.

The rational therapist, as noted above, insists on action as well as depropagandization, and often virtually or literally forces the client to do something to counteract his poor thinking. Adler wrote in this connection: "The actual change in the nature of the patient can only be his own doing" (4, p. 336).

Speaking of individuals with severe inadequacy feelings, Adler noted that "the proper treatment for such persons is to encourage them - never to discourage them" (2, p. 76). The rational therapist, more than virtually any other kind of psychotherapist, particularly gets at long-ingrained negative beliefs and philosophies by persuading, cajoling, and consistently encouraging the clients to be more constructive, more positive, more goal-oriented.

The rational therapist believes that human beings are not particularly affected by external people and things, but by the views they take of these things, and that they therefore have an almost unlimited power, through changing their sentences and their beliefs, to change themselves and to make themselves into almost anything they want. Said Adler in this connection: "We must make our own lives. It is our own task and we are capable of meeting it. We are masters of our own actions. If something new must be done or something old replaced, no one need do it but ourselves" (3, pp. 23-24).

DIFFERENCES FROM INDIVIDUAL PSYCHOLOGY

In many important respects, then, it should be obvious by now that rational psychotherapy and Individual Psychology overlap and support each other's tenets. There are, however, some significant differences. Although it has been reported (15) that Adler's therapeutic technique was often quite persuasive and even commanding, as the rational therapist's technique quite candidly is in many instances. Adler himself espoused a more passive view: "Special caution is called for in persuading the patient to any kind of venture. If this should come up, the consultant should say nothing for or against it, but, ruling out as a matter of course all generally dangerous undertakings, should only state that, while convinced of the success, he could not quite judge whether the patient was really ready for the venture" (4, p. 339).

It is mainly, however, in the realm of his views on social interest that Adler would probably take serious issue with the rational therapist. For the latter believes that rational human behavior primarily must be based on self-interest; and that, if it is so based, it will by logical necessity also have to be largely rooted in social interest. Adler seemed to believe the reverse: that only through a primary social interest could an individual achieve maximum self-love and happiness(4, p. 161; 3, p. 259).

Ansbacher and Ansbacher report in this connection: "To the most general formulation of the question, 'Why should I love my neighbor?', Adler is reported to have replied: 'If anyone asks me why he should love his neighbor, I would not know how to answer him, and I could only ask in my turn why he should pose such a question'" (4, p. 161). The rational therapist would tend to take a different stand and to say that there is a very good answer to the question of why one should love one's neighbor, or at least why one should take care not to harm him, namely, that only in so doing is one likely to help build the kind of society in which one would best live oneself. The rational therapist believes, in other words, that self-interest demands social interest; and that the rational individual who strives for his own happiness will, for that very reason, also be interested in others. Moreover, the rational therapist tends to believe, with Maslow (14)and other recent personality theorists, that the human animal normally and naturally is helpful and loving to other humans, provided that it is not enmeshed in illogical thinking that leads it to self-destructive, self-hating behavior.

Where Adler writes, therefore, that "All my efforts are devoted towards increasing the social interest of the patient" (3, p. 260), the rational therapist would prefer to say, "Most of my efforts are devoted towards increasing the self-interest of the patient." He assumes that if the individual possesses rational self-interest he will, on both biological and logical grounds, almost invariably tend to have a high degree of social interest as well.

CONCLUSION

In some theoretical ways, then, and in several specific elements of technique, which were not examined here for lack of space, rational psychotherapy and individual Psychology significantly differ. It is more interesting and important, however, to note the many ways in which they amazingly agree. That Alfred Adler should have had a half century start in stating some of the main elements of a theory of personality and psychotherapy which was independently derived from a rather different framework and perspective is indeed a remarkable tribute to his perspicacity and clinical judgment.

REFERENCES

1. ADLER, A. Understanding Human Nature. Near York: Greenberg, 1927.

2. ADLER, A. The science of living. New York: Greenberg, 1929.

3. ADLER, A. What life should mean to you. New York: Blue Ribbon Books, 1931.

4. ANSBACHER, H. L., & ANSBACHER, ROWENA R. (Eds.) The Individual Psychology of Alfred Adler. New York: Basic Books, 1956.

5. DUBOIS, P. The psychic treatment of nervous disorders. New York, Funk & Wagnalls 1907.

6. ELLIS, A. An introduction to the principles of scientific psychoanalysis. Genet. Psychol. Monogr., 1950, 41, 147-212.

7. ELLIS, A. New approaches to psychotherapy techniques. J. clin. Psychol. Monogr. Suppl., 1955, 11 207-260.

8. ELLIS, A. Psychotherapy techniques for use with psychotics. Amer. J. Psychother., 1955, 9, 452-476.

9. ELLIS, A. A critical evaluation of marriage counseling. Marr. Fam. living, 1956, 18, 65-71.

10. ELLIS, A. Rational Psychotherapy. Paper read at Amer. Psychol. Ass. Chicago, August, 1956. Also J. gen. Psychol., in presss.

11. EPICTETUS. The works of Epictetus. Transl. by T. W. Higginson. Boston: Little, Brown, 1899.

12. FREUD, S. Basic writings. New York: Modern Library, 1938.

13. FREUD, S. Collected Papers. London: Hogarth Press, 1924-1950.

14. MASLOW, A. H. Motivation and personality. New York: Harper, 1954.

15. MUNROE, RUTH. Schools of psychoanalytic thought. New York: Dryden Press 1955.

5. RECOLLECTIONS OF A PSYCHOANALYTIC PSYCHOTHERAPY: THE CASE OF "PRISONER K"

(Thomas Szasz 1959)

Fascinating account of "psychoanalytic psychotherapy" conducted by Thomas Szasz; who was soon to elevated into a position of international renown and controversy following the publication of his classic text "The Myth of Mental Illness."

"Psychoanalysis is not, in my opinion, in a position to create a Weltanschauung of its own. It has no need to do so, for it is a branch of science, and can subscribe to the scientific Weltanschauung." (S. Freud)

"I have assumed ... that psychoanalysis is not a specialized branch of medicine. I cannot see how it is possible to dispute this." (S. Freud)

On the Presentation of Psychoanalytic Treatment

Some Historical Considerations

To present the treatment process in the form of a complete account of the interaction of analyst and patient has been a keenly felt need ever since psychoanalysis became a distinct form of psychotherapeutic intervention. And yet no such account exists. Nor do I think it can be written. Freud said this much and regretfully likened the task of describing the technique of psychoanalysis to that of chess. Relying on this analogy, he thought that the most that could be done was to describe a few typical opening and closing "games" — and that the remainder would have to be learned in the course of one's work. In accordance with this thesis, the psychoanalytic literature contains only technical "rules" pertaining to the beginning and end phases of treatment. These are generally formulated in terms of technical maneuvers, such as the use of the couch, free association, the frequency of interviews, and other methods used in the beginning phase, or in terms of ideal abstractions, such as resolution of the transference neurosis or the "new beginning" used at the end of the: treatment. Rarely, if ever, are these notions illustrated by case material. What sort of psychoanalytic case material is there? In an overview of roughly a half-century of psychoanalysis, two types of material may be distinguished. First, there are excerpts of individual historical material presented to document a particular thesis concerning the patient's "psychopathology," its origin, its cause, and its "meaning." Second, there are accounts in which excerpts from clinical material are used to illustrate certain "therapeutic interventions" which resulted in what was judged to be "improvement." Many psychoanalytic contributions contain both types of material. This differentiation has been offered for purposes of clarification, and specifically to call attention to the prevalent aims motivating these reports. Breuer and Freud's original case reports in Studies on Hysteria offer a classic example of a work whose purpose was both to advance the thesis that historical events act as pathogenic agents and to show the efficacy of catharsis as a form of "therapy." Most of Freud's subsequent case histories are aimed primarily — sometimes solely (as in the Schreber case)— at presenting "psychopathology." Its medical counterpart, if any, would be an autopsy report. Turning now to more recent psychoanalytic contributions, it can be said that these generally have the same sort of goal as that which governed Breuer and Freud's original work — namely, to present evidence of a particular "conflict" or "disorder" and to describe how a specific therapeutic intervention resulted in an amelioration of it. To my knowledge, there is only one report of an "entire psychoanalysis." and it surely fails (in my opinion at least) to convey very much about the distinctive features of this form of psychotherapy. Instead, it, too, focused on exposing "psychopathology" and the nature of the "cure."

These considerations are mentioned to highlight the difference in emphasis which I propose to place in my presentation. I shall focus, in conformity with the general aims of this volume, on the nature of the therapeutic relationship. The material which I shall present is intended to convey a picture of the human relationship which existed between a {particular patient and myself-how it began, developed, and ended. The fact that the patient had certain "troubles" which caused him to initiate his contact with me is, of course, a part of the social reality within which our relationship developed. This, together with his (and my) expectation that we would be able to minimize his "troubles" as a result of our interaction with each other, is taken as the general socio-psychological matrix within which we worked. Beyond this, however, I have found that considerations of "sickness" and "health" do not enhance clarity of thought in this area and I have made an effort in this exposition, much as I do in my practical work, to avoid slipping into clichés borrowed from the medical model of treatment.

Selection of Material and Method

It is well known that the publication of case material obtained in psychotherapeutic practice presents certain difficulties. Most important among these are the need to preserve the patient's anonymity and the need for discretion in the way of self-disclosure on the therapist's part. In attempting to organize a presentation of my own style of working with patients, I encountered some additional problems. First, the matter of anonymity imposed a special problem because a relatively large proportion of my patients have been professional men and women, many of them physicians. This, of course, is true for the practice of many analysts nowadays. I mention it because it necessitated the exclusion of the majority of my patients from among those whose treatment, no matter how disguised, I wished to consider for presentation. The next problem, also a typical one for psychoanalysis, was that I kept no notes about my work with patients! In other words, I have no record that would bring to mind the specific sequential patterns so characteristic of the analytic process. I write an occasional note after an interview, and sometimes even during one, but these usually have more to do with my current interests than with any special therapeutic relevance of the event or thought.

In view of these circumstances, the account which follows is based very largely on my recollections. Moreover, in order further to insure the patient's anonymity, I have selected the therapy of a man who first came to see me nearly a decade ago. We saw each other for two and a half years and have had no contact since then. Accordingly, my memory is not exactly fresh concerning many of the details of this treatment. It is worth noting, also, that my style of working has changed somewhat during the intervening years. This, I think, is an unavoidable occurrence in the life of every therapist, reflecting as it does not only his own learning of his "trade" (if indeed such learning has occurred) but also changes in his personal life, meaning thereby both his external and internal object relationships. Against these difficulties which stand in the way of reproducing a relatively accurate account of this therapeutic relationship, there stand two factors which have helped to recapture it. First, I made and saved a few notes concerning various aspects of the patient's chief "symptoms" and their communicational meanings as these emerged in the course of the treatment. Secondly, I found that in the course of preparing this report, I was able to recall a large number of events.

From what I have said, it should be evident that the therapeutic experience which I shall describe is not offered as a typical - or ideal - sample of what "psychoanalysis" is, or ought to be. It is presented rather as an account of a particular instance or example of "psychoanalytic psychotherapy." Various features of this patient's personality and some of the circumstances of the therapy have made for some differences between this treatment and what could be regarded as the theoretical model of psychoanalysis. I might add, however, that I consider the "ideal psychoanalytic model of treatment" as something analogous to the "ideal gas" of physics. That is to say, it is a theoretical model which helps us to conceptualize a process and thus serves as a guide in our daily work. The laws governing the behavior of "ideal gases" provide an abbreviated description of the behavior of vaporized substances under very special conditions. The fact that these special conditions cannot usually be reproduced does not deprive this model from a great measure of usefulness under conditions which only approximate those of an "ideal gas." Similarly, while we strive to approximate the model of the "ideal analysis" as far as the patient's condition and our own knowledge and ability permit, we realize that it is something of a rarity.

The nature of psychoanalysis as "treatment" lends itself more readily to a theoretical than to a clinical description and I have presented my views on this subject elsewhere. To illustrate these principles by means of clinical material, it would be necessary — at the very least — to recapture the sequential evolution of an analytic relationship. As I have mentioned, I had never attempted to do this. And I doubt whether it could be done. Others, perhaps, may try it someday. There is considerable interest in this general subject at present and numerous "research projects" have been designed to record the analytic relationship in a form which will make it available to others for examination and study. It has become fashionable to sound-record psychiatric (and even so-called psychoanalytic) interviews and attempts are being made to both sound-record and film an entire "analysis." I think these devices, by means of which investigators seek to convert the privacy of the analytic relationship into "public data," miss the very problem which concerns us here and thereby distract attention from its eventual clarification.

Without entering into the complexities of this issue, I wish to make my point of view clear. I consider the analytic relationship to be a private matter between the two participating persons. This is what is meant by a two-person situation. No one else can enter into it or share it. It is similar, in this regard, to other significant human relationships, though in certain ways it is different from any of them. I would therefore compare the analytic relationship to the relationship with one's mother, father, brother, wife, friend, and so forth. None of these could be captured, so to speak, for public examination by, for instance, recording everything that went on between the participants. An even simpler, and therefore better, example of the privacy of this type of data is the relationship between a spectator and the Rembrandt masterpiece he is contemplating. His experience of beauty can in no way (that we know about) be recorded. It is a private matter between him and his object. There is, however, a relatively simple means by which we can gain access to this material, namely, by communicating with him. Accordingly, if we wish to learn about a human relationship, we must communicate with the participants in it. When we ourselves are the participant in a relationship, we are in a position to disclose certain things about it to others. It seems to me that what we are not prepared to reveal, others will have a difficult time finding out. In other words, what analysts or other psychotherapists withhold concerning their activities with patients, cameras and sound- recorders may not succeed in uncovering. True, it may be possible to disclose with this technique some happenings not otherwise "admitted," but the alteration of the privacy of the two-person situation complicates our task to such an extent that there is reason for grave doubts about where this method will lead us.

The most accurate method of rendering human relationships "public" is, of course, that of the novelist. Indeed, we regard it as his distinctive task to portray human relationships from the inside, as it were. Clearly, it is easier, psychologically, to do this with hypothetical people than with' real ones, particularly when the "real person" is oneself. Nevertheless, some biographies, and also a few autobiographies, do manage to convey the human drama which is their subject with amazing fidelity. Viewed in this light, recounting the story of an analysis in toto would call for the skills of a novelist and a book the length of a sizable novel. Moreover, if the widest I possible coverage of this interpersonal relationship were desired, it would be necessary to obtain descriptions of the interaction from both participants: analyst and patient. Attempts of this sort, while not without difficulties, would offer more promise, in my opinion, than recordings or other attempts at pseudo-objectification of analysis. Short of such novelistic efforts, which require gigantic investments of interest and knowledge, analysts can contribute to the task of making their work available to others by the publication of fragments of analyses and by descriptions of the essential features of their work. It is my hope that the following fragmentary account of my work with a patient will furnish a glimpse into what is otherwise a private, or two-person situation.

The Unfolding of the Therapeutic Relationship and of the Patient's History and Personal Identity in it

"Someone must have been telling lies about Joseph K., for without having done anything wrong he was arrested one fine morning." (Franz Kafka)

In searching for a pseudonym for my patient, it occurred to me to call him simply "K.," the designation which Franz Kafka used for his hero in The Castle and The Trial The theme of these novels revolves around Kafka's struggles with his introjected objects, mainly his parents. "K.," the protagonist, represents, without much doubt, the author himself. With real artistic skill, Kafka conveyed his feelings of being guilty of some wrong- doing, his pervasive sense of "being at fault," and of futility and impending doom. The similarity of his personal tribulations and feelings and my patient's occurred to me during the treatment and we discussed it on many occasions. It thus seems logical now to call my patient "K." and specifically to direct the reader's attention to the many significant similarities between the hero of The Castle and The Trial on the one hand, and my patient on the other. In Kafka's case we know, too, how he had tried to heal himself, so to speak, through an unusual kind of love relationship, his adoption of fanatical Zionism as a "cause," and last but not least through his artistic creativity — and how all these had failed to do more than temporarily stave off his tragic demise. My efforts to interpose psychoanalytic influence in an attempt to alter and ameliorate my patient's similar drift toward tragedy and doom may be viewed in the light of this background. Yet, we cannot ascertain from the later developments of my patient how effective or ineffective my efforts were, for I have had no contact with him, nor any news about him, since our last meeting. It was not my intent, however, to relate an historical account of a patient and his subsequent life, and so I ask the reader to be satisfied with the material at my command.

Beginning of the Treatment

"K." was a man of mature years engaged in a complicated profession for which he had undergone prolonged training and preparation. His intelligence was superior, his appearance was pleasant, and his interest in helping himself through analysis, once he embarked upon it, was both earnest and persistent. He was unmarried and had practically no friends. Although he was veritably alone, he did not feel lonely. He was friendly, and had many superficial personal relationships, all of them harmonious. He held himself back, almost consciously, however, from any personal involvements. His main interest was his work. Much attention, of course, had to be paid to keeping himself uninvolved in various human relationships for which opportunities constantly arose. This feature of his personality, that is, his single-minded defense against new object relationships, became evident as he described himself during the first several interviews, and it was an important reason why he had not sought psychoanalytic help earlier. For many years he had had conscious thoughts about seeking treatment, vaguely desired it, but never did anything about it. He was, of course, painfully aware of his dangerous symptom: exhibitionism, but sought to "control" it by himself. When questioned about his reluctance to seek therapy earlier, he was puzzled and could give no explanation for it. It was as if something — an invisible hand — had held him back, much as he was held back from any and all human relationships which required a measure of psychological commitment on his part.

It seemed to me that the manner in which he finally entered into the therapeutic situation had something to do with the pattern sketched above. This impression grew and gained support from various historical determinants as the story of his life unfolded.

The specific circumstances under which "K." began treatment follow. He was arrested by the police for "indecent exposure." As soon as he came before the judge for this offense, it was suggested to him that, if he were to seek psychiatric help, charges would be held pending, and would perhaps be dismissed later. He seized upon this opportunity to seek psychotherapy. Nor was this particular outcome of his arrest surprising to him. Rather, it was as if he had expected it. Accordingly, there existed the possibility that his arrest was largely self-determined and had certain purposive aspects. Among these, its meaning as a desperate, yet disguised, cry for help seemed immediately apparent and relevant. This conjecture was supported by the fact that the patient had had the impulse to exhibit himself for many years, and had done so on rare occasions, but had never been apprehended for it.

I might note, in this connection, that much of the therapy was concerned with filling in all of the minute details of his exhibitionism, meaning thereby its antecedents, his thoughts and affects at the time and thereafter, the effects on others and himself, and so forth. This should not imply that; this was the main focus of our work, or that he was directed to concentrate his attention on this topic. Nor does it mean that this was done with a "cathartic" aim, that is, that by verbalizing as much as possible about this symptom and its probable determinants, he was to be "cured" of it. Instead of these points of view, the one by which I was governed, and to which I still adhere in my work, was that a full view of this area of his life, and of many other areas, help both the patient and me to see what sort of person he is. The unfolding of the 'history" is therefore regarded as the process by which the patient's "identity" comes into focus in "the open," where both he and I can look at it. This, in turn, is done as a prerequisite for seeing how he has lived and how he continues to conduct himself. In the light of this knowledge, and armed by it, the patient achieves a measure of mastery and control over his previously unconscious object relationships. He is then in a better position to decide for himself how he wants to alter his own "identity," partly by altering his own internal objects ("working through"), and partly by a more conscious, and if necessary cautious, selection of his external object relationships. This digression is offered here to explain why much of the material that follows is in the nature of sociohistorical data about this patient. I shall intersperse comments concerning certain therapeutic activities on my part and observations relevant to the analytic situation proper. This mode of presentation obviously will not recreate the continuity of the original therapeutic process, nor is it intended to achieve that goal. It is hoped, rather, that it will recapture the continuity of a recollection which, after all, is the source of this account.

In the initial period of my acquaintance with "K.," he was mortified by shame because of his symptom. He also felt humiliated and "dirty." He went to some lengths to reassure me that his desire for "help" was genuine and not motivated solely by the legal compulsion to undertake it. There then began the self-disclosure which characterizes the early phases of most analyses: the endless details concerning parental behavior, homes, meals, schools attended, exploits and frustrations, and so forth. Other "symptoms" were mentioned. He was afraid of "homosexuality." Why was he not married? He had no interest in marriage and could not imagine himself with a wife and children. He had sexual interest in prostitutes. Occasionally he befriended these girls and then had a remote kind of personal and sexual relationship with them. The girls looked upon him as a friend and he did not pay them, although he knew that they had other partners who did.

He formerly had a speech impediment ("stuttering"). It had begun at about puberty, and it had been most pronounced when he spoke to his parents. I saw no sign of it. Nor had he any trouble in speaking to others this time. Later, when I became an object of more importance and one with whom he had conflicts, this symptom reappeared in the therapeutic situation.

He had a fear of venereal disease, particularly syphilis, but he believed that he could control this fear. His main sexual activity was masturbation, which he regarded as "very infantile," words he used to mean that it was "bad." He regarded the urge to masturbate as "compulsive" because he could not stop it. Gradually, there emerged a picture of himself as a "growing kid."

His parents did not really take him seriously. They were ever "helpful," "interested," and "kind" — but this was their role in the real-life play in which they were acting. The parents acted the roles of "good," solicitous, nature "adults"; the patient's role was that of the failing son. He was an only child. Early in life he found his life-role in the family defined for him n the Kafkaesque style to which I referred earlier. Both parents were intelligent and highly educated. Their education, however, was a symbol and substitute for achievement in other areas. According to the patient's account, they were deeply unfulfilled. Their ambitions to do creative work were never achieved. They rationalized their failings with near-psychotic fictions: past illnesses which required physical care at the expense of intensive effort, social non-recognition, ill luck, and last but not least, theirs need to sacrifice themselves for their son's upbringing. In accordance with these parental needs, "K.'s" childhood development took a particular turn. He developed an inner sense of two separate identities, or perhaps, two trends toward separate roles. One role was complementary to his parents — mostly his mother's — behavior toward him. This necessitated perseverance with good behavior and important adult achievements as goals toward which he should strive but never reach. Illustrative of this pattern is the following episode which occurred when the patient was in his thirties. Following his participation in an event which was socially regarded as an achievement, his mother inquired whether he was sorry that he had not pursued another activity which he had abandoned long ago. While his mother knew about his current achievement, she behaved as though she were totally unaware of it. And, in fact, there was good reason to assume that this was not an "act" in the sense of a deliberately contrived performance, but rather that it reflected the mother's thorough-going repression or denial of these events.

The other direction in which his feeling of self (or identity) developed was much less clear-cut. There was merely a very vague and uncertain feeling that the "self" described above, which was the dominant and consciously experienced one, was somehow not all that there was to him. This "inner self" was merely a minute fragment of his total personality, a fragment that was kept uncontaminated by his parents. It was formed on the basis of his identifications with others—a sensible cousin here, a friend's criticism of his mother there, and so forth—and could be regarded as a vestige of his "unmodified ego." There was, finally, an element of the well-known split of the ego into observing and experiencing portions (or aspects) which was reflected in these two "identities." The bad, guilty, Kafkaesque self was the experiencing and acting "K."; his "inner self," though mostly absent, was sometimes the observer, disassociated from the behavior it saw.

The first several months of the treatment led to the unfolding of the patient's picture of himself as a terribly disordered, "cursed" individual. Father used to say, sarcastically, that he was a carbon copy of his mother. What did this mean? It meant, chiefly, that the patient was terribly mentally disturbed, as the father (correctly) considered the mother to be. It also meant that father disapproved of him. Since the father was weak and helpless vis-a-vis his wife, he could express his dissatisfactions with her only by using his son as a substitute victim. And, of course, it meant man) other things pertinent to the family homeostasis which was maintained by' the particular ways in which father, mother, and "K." related to each other. The quintessence of this family's image of itself was that the mother had to think of herself as a supremely successful "mother" and "wife." This was to be her solace for all her frustrations in life, which included the loss of her own mother (i.e., "K.'s" maternal grandmother) early in life and other terrible blows from which she never recovered. Indeed, her solution seemed to be, at least after her marriage, to make no effort to meet problems and come to grips with them. Instead, she would overcome all obstacles through make-believe maneuvers. In these tragi-comic substitute-masteries she was supported by her husband, and later by "K." Only after a considerable length of time in therapy were various pieces of this picture of "K.'s" mother illuminated by his recollections. Mother had innumerable personal peculiarities related to eating, family relationships, social events, and so forth. These were confined, for the most part, within tier own household, and thus never led to social or psychiatric complications, so to speak. Yet they were evident enough, so much so that several of the patient's more distant relatives had stated unequivocally that she was "crazy." Many would refuse to visit in her house. Yet the patient had tried to repress and deny these perceptions of his mother. The reasons that tie had to repudiate this threatening "reality" and thereby falsify his own sense of himself and of everything about him were basically twofold. First, as long as he lived at home, in the role of a child dependent on his parents, le obviously could not admit to himself that his life was in the hands of such unreachable and, indeed, partly malevolent persons. Fairbairn has aptly compared this problem of the child to the religious dichotomy of God and devil. It is safer for man (child) to believe that he himself is bad, or that he is possessed by the devil but with a benevolent God's care assured for his needs than to contemplate a world governed by the devil, the introjection of the parent's "badness" is a typical solution of this psychological dilemma. "K." had been exposed to precisely this type of trauma, one that probably is not at all uncommon and plays a particularly important part in personality developments with marked psychotic proclivities." The second reason for the development of "K.'s" view of his parents, and of his whole world, may be said to have originated in the world-view which he had been taught. Inasmuch as it is the parents who generally define for the child what his environment (human and otherwise) is like, he latter's so-called "distortion of reality" may be considered to stem, partly, from the discrepancy between the grown child's (or "patient's") and the observer's respective "educations."

The World of Internal Objects

"K." related a number of striking incidents in connection with his relationship to his mother, of which I remember only a few. An outstanding memory of his was of an occurrence when he was about 7 or 8 years old. Shortly after coming home from school one day, something occurred which made him feel very displeased with his mother and he angrily shouted, "I hate you." His mother's response to this was devastating. She acted as though she had literally collapsed, almost as though he had beaten her nearly to death. "K.'s" father had to "explain" later that "K." "really did not mean it" and that he loved her. He himself had to "apologize" and promise that he would never say such a thing again as long as he lived. The implication of all this was clear enough. Mother could not be challenged in her concept of herself as someone always good and lovable. And, of course, "K." received the impression that he had tremendous power over her, and others, and that he must be careful not to hurt anyone. He dated the beginning of the intense feelings that he was "peculiar," different from others, somehow unalterably "bad," from this event. His stuttering, too, began shortly afterwards and, as I mentioned, was most pronounced when he had to speak with his parents! A related event occurred sometime later when his father was said to have suffered a coronary occlusion. However, he never again had any trouble referable to this illness. Indeed, from all that could be learned from the patient's recollections there was considerable doubt about whether this diagnosis was correct, or whether it formed a part of his parents' defensive operations against psychological inroads on them. In any case, from his early adolescence it was impressed upon "K." that he must be very careful in what he said and did, lest by his actions he hurt his parents. He was thus made to learn certain rules of conduct, based however on principles that were to some extent self-contradictory. These were, briefly, as follows: (1) His parents were all-loving, good, wise, and very powerful. He had to do what they wanted I him to do, for they alone knew what was best for him. (2) His parents were also extremely weak and fragile, but this was not to be dwelled upon Thus his mother could not stand criticism of any sort and his father might die of a heart attack at any time (if he misbehaved). Father also had no control over mother's "peculiarities," but instead of admitting his limitations in this regard, he acted as though there was nothing whatever in her behavior that he disliked. (3) He — "K." — was a little boy full of malicious destructiveness which had to be controlled and disguised by his parents', and his own, educational efforts. These efforts, of course, were destined to fail, but they must at least try their best to inhibit his proclivity toward "badness."

Although "K." had been vaguely aware of many things about the family situation in which he grew up, his adult life, prior to his coming into treatment, was conducted in such a way that he diverted himself from looking straight at these facts, historical as well as current. He regarded the psychotherapeutic situation as his first opportunity to pour out his soul. Yet, he did this with a measure of detachment. It was striking that he always avoided any open criticism of his parents. What he did was to present certain occurrences and then let either the "facts speak for themselves," or, as an alternative, he waited for the analyst to make some comment. It soon became apparent that he was still afraid to speak ill of his parents. When this assumption was communicated to him, he agreed. At this point, his speech became noticeably affected and he manifested an irregular stuttering for many months. Outside of his relationship with me, however, his speech remained unaffected.

His fear of hurting his parents was impressive. That he wished to hurt them, he knew, of course, but yet he did not do so. It is difficult to describe these psychological events in ordinary English, or any other language, since the logic of our everyday language does not permit the expression of layerings or "polyvalences" of affects, and of object relationships, as these actually occur in human relationships. Instead, we can express only a single, monovalent affect or relationship in one sentence, and must follow it (in temporal and spatial sequence) by another, and then by still another "layer" of the same relationship. We should at least be cognizant of this linguistic limitation which is responsible for a great difficulty in correctly describing certain human events. Thus, when we say that someone was conscious of something, we imply that he was not also unconscious of some other aspects of this same thing. Yet we know that combinations of such states are in fact the rule. Similarly, the concept of "denial" implies fairly total unawareness—yet denial and a certain kind of awareness tend to coexist. So much for this problem of the limitations of ordinary language for the scientific description of human affects and relationships.

"K.'s" fear of expressing disapproval of his parents manifested itself in numerous ways. His overt relationship to them was completely "harmonious." He never criticized them, never disagreed with them, and tried always to do what they requested. Yet he held himself aloof and tried to escape from them by placing geographical distance between himself and them. This maneuver was a substitute for any more overt attempt to separate himself from them. He felt, of course, that he could not openly do this, for his parents would regard it as an affront and a reproach indicating that they were not as good as they had thought they were. Then they would get sick and die, and he would be "responsible." Above all, he did not want to be "responsible."

"K." had had a long-standing fantasy which he related during our discussions of his relationship with his parents. It condensed and expressed his problem with them in a striking manner. He imagined himself driving his car, being forced off the street by a truck, and hitting and injuring (killing?) a child. His guilt, even in the fantasy, was intense. Yet he would tell himself that it was not his fault! He was forced into this situation. Then he would tell himself that he could still not blame anyone else. When I connected the fantasy with his relationship with his parents, a connection which he had never been able to make himself, he agreed enthusiastically that this was exactly the difficulty. He could not blame his parents for any wrongdoing. It would be terribly ungrateful to do so, after the way they had stood by him, no matter what he would do. The meaning of this fantasy is, I believe, self-explanatory in the light of what has been said. In this connection, "K." also related a persistent feeling which he had had ever since his teens and which consisted of a dread of doing some unalterable wrong. What the "wrong" would be was vague; nor was it important to him. What was important was, as he put it, "... that the memory of the defection will always be there ... you can never make it up." He was filled with a constant anticipation of being apprehended — for what he did not know. When he was, finally, arrested at least this sense of uncertainty — namely, for what he would be arrested — disappeared. The apprehension about being arrested for some wrongdoing persisted, however. Intimately connected with it was the feeling that he was "not guilty." Also there was the notion that he would not be able to convince anyone that he was innocent.

As his relationship with his parents became increasingly clear and explicit, he gradually freed himself of his fears of them. His inhibitions in relation to them also diminished. His own need for his parents, due partly to his continued dependence on them and partly to his essentials "objectlessness," was deeply buried beneath his conviction that his parents needed him (which was also true).

Two important "external" events occurred during the first year of treatment, before - I might add - many of the ramified meanings and functions of his chief symptom, exhibitionism, could be elucidated.

The first was that the patient's probationary period expired. In connection with this topic he developed marked anxieties and extensive fantasies. Outstanding was the fear of the "record" of his misdeed. He felt that this would always hang over him like the sword of Damocles. He would never be able to get rid of this record. How could he ever get married now? How could he pursue his work, and carry on his usual activities? He thought that even if, with the help of treatment, he could rid himself of his exhibitionism, this would, in the end, do him no good. He would be doomed by his "record." Fantasies such as these led to comparisons between himself and Kafka's hero in The Castle and The Trial. And, in turn, it slowly became possible for him to see that the "record" that sentenced him to everlasting doom was a vision of his parents, as "bad objects," who continued to control him. Only after extensive working through of his relationship to his parents (as internal objects), did it become possible for him to approach the matter of the "record" realistically.

It then developed that since his offense was never legally "confirmed," the record of his arrest had been destroyed. We have slipped ahead of our narrative, however. As the end of his probationary period approached, the question of what sort of contact I would have with the legal authorities arose. On the one hand, he wanted me to intercede on his behalf; on the other, he wished, as I believe all (adult) patients do, that I should have no contact with anyone in regard to him. He asked what I would do. I told him that my position was (and is) to have no contact with anyone but the patient with whom I work, and I indicated that I thought a stand of non- involvement could be maintained in his case, too. This turned out to be true. When the appointed time came for "K." to speak to the legal authorities again, he appeared on the scene armed with competent legal aid, and succeeded without trouble in having all charges against him dropped. He had, apparently, no difficulty convincing the authorities that he was in treatment with me, for I was never even contacted to confirm this fact.

These events proved - then and during subsequent months - to have been exceedingly important not only "realistically" (as they indeed were) but also in certain symbolic-communicative ways. What I have in mind is this. The "legal problem" had come up, now and again, during the initial months of the analysis. Both of us knew that at the end of the probationary period further legal action would be taken. It seemed likely, of course, that the charges against "K." would simply be dropped, thus ending the legal phase of this matter. But "K." could not convince himself that this was likely to happen. Accordingly, he felt quite outnumbered, so to speak, by the legal forces which he believed were pitted against him, and he sought for an ally in me, I pointed this out to him. We also discussed the possibility that he might engage an attorney if what he wanted was literally an "ally." He continued to speculate, however, about how my testimony on his behalf might be helpful to him. It was my impression at the time, and this became amply confirmed later, that had I consented to his wishes, this would have resulted in a catastrophic situation in the treatment. It probably would have led to the acting out of his exhibitionism and a breakdown of the treatment, since a repetition and re-enactment of the original pathogenic family situation would have been fostered in his relationship to me. For if I had consented to "help him out," and if I had written or spoken to the appropriate people as he wished me to do, telling them that "K." was in treatment with me and doing well, I certainly would have communicated to him the following adventitious messages as well. First, since I had tried to "help" him in this way, it must prove that he was indeed as bad and sinful as he had thought he was; without my help, there was no telling what would have happened. Second, he might have thought, and I believe correctly, that I, as a psychiatrist, was merely an extension of the law-enforcement agencies of society. What would I do in case he again exhibited himself? Would I report it to the police? Would I continue to treat him? These questions, I might add, never actually arose. I am merely suggesting that they would have arisen had I assumed the "role" of (a) protecting him from the police and (b) protecting society (in collaboration with the police) from him. As it happened, I adhered to the role to which I like to adhere (unless, as rarely happens, I can convince myself that there are other relevant factors which justify a departure from it), namely, trying to help "K." by "analyzing" him. By this term I refer to the process of assisting the patient to acquire as clear a picture of himself and of his human relationships as is possible, thus enabling him to decide for himself how he wants to change. If this endeavor is successful, the patient usually finds it possible to implement his wishes effectively, for he is no longer constrained by conflicting goals arising from his unconscious relationships to internal objects.

The second important event, occurring during the first year, was that the treatment was to be interrupted for several weeks during my summer vacation. Prior to this time, the therapeutic work had been "going well" in the sense that "K." had been successful—and without undue anxiety on his part or upheavals in his actual life situation—in consistently enlarging his grasp over the historical and psychological determinants of his relationship with people. The connections between these object relationships and his chief symptoms became progressively clearer. It was during this period, which "K." felt had been so useful to him, that my vacation was to interrupt the therapy. He was, of course, unhappy about it. We discussed the fact that the vacation came in the middle of his treatment and that the interruption was an unpleasant prospect for him. Much of this discussion occurred several weeks before my departure from the city, when I first communicated my vacation plans to him. Then for weeks we went along much as before. On the day of our last meeting until after my vacation, "K." reported a dream. He had relatively few dreams, and dream-analysis occupied only a very small part of our previous work. The dream had occurred the night before this interview. It was a "nightmare," in which he felt horribly anxious, and awoke feeling as though he had been "through a wringer." The dream was simply this: "A crime had been committed. ..." He added that he did not know what the crime was, or who committed it.

Before reporting the dream, "K." began the hour by speaking about his exhibitionism. He reviewed how he had been feeling and concluded that he had felt quite free of any impulses in that direction. But, he added, he wondered whether he was, or could be, "really cured" of exhibitionism Then he related the dream. Without going into unnecessary details, I will add only one more factor for consideration before commenting on the meaning of the dream. It is simply that it was quite clear to both "K." and me that the treatment was not far enough advanced, at this time, to have freed him sufficiently from this symptom. He felt its disappearance depended, in good measure, on the therapeutic relationship, and that it did not yet lie as within himself. I agreed with his appraisal of the situation. We proceeded to discuss this in the light of the following interpretation which I had placed on the dream.

It seemed to me that the dream occurred in response to a seriously threatening disturbance in the therapeutic situation. My departure promised to leave "K." alone, perhaps unable to cope with his "bad" internal objects and/or sexual impulses, which threatened him because of their ego- alien, socially-alien, and self-destructive potentialities. In the dream, and by reporting it to me, "K." had addressed me something as follows: "What will happen to me when you leave ... ? This ... [crime (exhibitionism)]... is what might happen! Please do not leave." That this should have been communicated in dream form, rather than more directly, was due, I believe, to the fact that the patient's conscious ego, which was in many ways mature and very capable, could not fully endure the thought (1) that he might still be so vulnerable to his internal objects and unconscious impulses, and (2) that he was so dependent on me for help. Thus the dream was viewed as an indirect communication, both to himself and to me. To himself, "K." spoke of the danger facing him indirectly — "What crime? By whom?" To me, he spoke of his vulnerability, and hence of my responsibility. "What crime and by whom?" in this connection, may have meant the therapist and his leaving.

All this we discussed. He made no suggestion that I should stay, nor did I offer to change my plans. Clearly, there was a measure of risk either in leaving or in staying. This I did not discuss with "K." then, although I think I did, in retrospect, much later in the treatment. What I have in mind is that if I had acknowledged his plea for support and stayed, I would have corroborated his own fear of being unable to control himself. This was, and is, the danger in any therapeutic tendency (in analysis) toward assuming a so-called "protective" role. On the other hand, there was danger also in the course of action which I took. While it tended to convey to him, implicitly, not only that I "trusted" him, but more significantly that I thought he was "safe" enough until my return, it also exposed him to the danger of a recurrence of real-life (i.e., social and legal) difficulties. Let me emphasize that I do not believe the matter of "trusting" the patient was of primary importance here — although many therapists lay stress on it — because our relationship was not based on his having to please me by "behaving properly." Hence there was no issue of either trusting or not trusting him. Our relationship was in no way conditional upon his "good" behavior — except, of course, for the fact that he had to be available to come to my office. It was, therefore, understood that if he were to break any laws and end up in jail, which he had fantasized occasionally, then I could not treat him. It did not seem to me that there was need for me to implement this "condition" of the analysis with "threats" of my own. In fact, to have done so would have been quite foreign to my orientation to this problem. Last but not least, contemplating what effects such behavior on my part would have had on "K.," I could not help but feel that he would have interpreted it as an excessive, and wholly unnecessary, attempt on my part to control him. If he was hypersensitive about anything it was this, and perhaps he made me hypersensitive in turn to his own needs for maximum self-determination compatible with the needs of the task at hand. I might add, however, that it seems to me that most patients who are oriented to treatment by analysis desire to have their self-determination encroached on as little as possible as a result of treatment.

As it turned out, "K.'s" life during the interruption of the treatment was uneventful.

We continued to deal with the various historical determinants of his self-concept. On occasion he had "obsessive" thoughts, such as "What would happen if I did something peculiar?" "Peculiar" meant overt homosexual activity, exhibitionism, and, later, various other anti-social acts. His first thoughts turned to the fear of losing control over himself or his "impulses." By having such thoughts consciously he was also testing himself, showing himself that indeed he was not doing any of these things. But why should he? His mother, we learned, showed much interest in his sexual development and, later, in what she fantasized might be his sexual activities. This began with her compulsive attention to where he kept his hands during sleeping, a pattern which dated back as far as "K." could remember. In this case, as in other situations, "K.'s" mother claimed that she was acting on behalf of her son's best interests. He should keep his hands outside the covers, or else he will have the most terrible nightmares. As "K." neared puberty — or perhaps he only noticed it then — he became aware that his parents were exceedingly demonstrative with each other in his presence. They acted like newlyweds. This embarrassed him. In looking back during the analysis, "K." thought this fitted into the pattern of his parents' acting the role of the perfectly mated couple. They were ecstatically happy with each other, and were the perfect parents for him. Accordingly, as "K." became a teenager, they were anxious for him to be "maximally normal." Actually, as with themselves, this meant that he should act the role of social normality. This role, they were evidently convinced, was the proper cover-up for the terrible "abnormalities" that must lie hidden in the deeper recesses of his personality (as they felt was the case with them). "K.'s" parents, and particularly his mother, gave many overt expressions of this morbid preoccupation. She wanted to know if he had girl friends and passionately encouraged his "dating" activities. This lesson, so to speak, was deeply impressed upon "K." and he used to have many dates. He proved to his mother — and, of course, also to himself (the difference was a matter of viewpoint and emphasis) — that he was 'normal." This dating-pattern played an important part in triggering off his occasional exhibitionistic acts. Later in his teens, his mother began to speak more openly of her fears that he would become a homosexual. Whenever she read of some sexual crime in the newspapers, she would muse about how terrible it would be (for her, that is!) if her beloved son, "K.," developed such proclivities. She thus treated sexual deviation as some mysterious plague which might be visited upon anyone at any time, but particularly as some divine punishment visited upon parents via the perverted behavior of their grown children. She could, indeed, never learn to regard "K." as a separate human being. She viewed him either as a part of herself, her "bad" self, or else she tended to confuse him with others, mainly her husband (who was still another part of her). She often made slips of the tongue and called "K." by the wrong name. She could never remember the names of any of his friends. These are merely samples of the innumerable recollections which "K." started to have once he was able to look at his mother (and father). He was thus forced to conclude that, at least in her relationship to him, her orientation was an essentially "psychotic" one.

She would say, for example, that if "K." were to become a homosexual, she would kill herself. "K.," of course, became increasingly angry, and somewhat depressed, as he began to realize that these reconstructions of his family life must eventuate in the loss of his parents. In fact, he now had to lose them twice. First, he had to lose them as the "good" parents that he imagined them to have been. Second, having revised his ideas about them, and himself, he had to lose them as the "real objects" that they were; for, as he now saw them, he was of course no longer interested in having very much to do with them. The mobilization of this real-life conflict, with which he had never dealt before (as it could not previously have assumed this shape), he attributed, correctly, to the therapy. And he was angry at me for it. Traces of his resentment over this never quite left him— or so it seemed to me. Perhaps this is the sort of phenomenon to which Freud referred when he spoke about the patient having to face, as a result of analysis, the realistic unhappiness of life.

Yet, it never seemed to me that he was really dissatisfied with this turn of events. It was evident, too, that he would have preferred that his symptoms could be removed somehow without the necessity of any changes in his ideas concerning, or behavior toward, any actual persons. Thus, he would have preferred to view his exhibitionism, and all sorts of bad impulses in himself, as his very private "badness," due solely to his "innate sins" (due perhaps to "genetics"), which somehow should be removed (as by a surgical operation). He thus desired, at least initially, to be "himself without his badness." The possibility that his "badness" was at once himself and not himself, in the sense of it having been learned by his antecedent human relationships, made him feel uncomfortable. He was especially unhappy to assume that his parents affected him as I thought they perhaps did. For, if they did, they might still do so, and this would necessitate changing his relationship to them. This he still feared. It was in this connection that once again we could discuss and "work through" his fears that he might destroy them. His anxiety on this score was, in turn, nurtured by his repressed rage. Each of these affects and orientations of his was discussed with him only as he actually experienced them and complained about them.

Although "K." was a man of mature years, he was peeved at me because when he felt a need to separate himself from his parents he experienced what he called a feeling of "disloyalty" toward them. This, among other things, was a defense against his facing the trauma of separation. He was torn between feeling "bad and dirty" but secure in his object-relationship with his parents, on the one hand, and the possibility of acquiring an improved sense of self-esteem together with a measure of at least initial loneliness and personal insecurity, on the other hand. I pointed this out to him. His feeling of "disloyalty," however, expressed also his own peculiar fear of the world, which he shared with his parents. The three of them had developed a Weltanschauung similar to the narcissistic-paranoid orientation of some small nations. This may be paraphrased as follows: "We are a small group of exceptional people, supremely loyal to one another, who are surrounded and threatened by an alien, inferior, and destructive world." This self- aggrandizing fiction, of course, is extremely effective as long as it works. And it tends to work as long as the person directs his chief expectations toward members of the in-group and does not associate with outsiders. This was still true for "K.," while he was in treatment, and this, too, was a subject for our discussion. He really had no persons other than his parents from whom he expected anything, except, that is, me. This was the main reason, of course, why he listened to me and was in fact so interested in being involved in "disloyalty" to his parents. In other words, I offered him something which he could not get from his "own group," in spite of all of their bragging about their own greatness. The more I could prove my usefulness to him, the more convinced he became that he did not need his parents, as he had previously believed.

In this connection we touch on the complex matter of his feelings of "badness" and how it nevertheless guaranteed an exalted status for him, at least in the world as he had pictured it. It was necessary, therefore, not only for him to realize that perhaps he was not as "bad" as he thought he was, but also that he needed to revise his opinions about the exceptional and exalted nature of his parents, and indirectly also of himself. This sounds like a logical contradiction, and in logic it would be a contradiction. Yet, in psychology such antithetical beliefs, self-concepts, and affects are not only non-contradictory, but are in fact common, if not invariable, occurrences.

Thus, behind "K.'s" feelings of worthlessness and sinfulness, there lay an equally intense feeling of self-importance and sense of exceptionalness. In this, too, he showed a great similarity to Kafka's literary hero and, of course, to Kafka himself.

Exhibitionism as an Experience

Let us now return to "K.'s" chief symptom, exhibitionism, and see what we learned about it. Sometime after the first few months of treatment, "K." would mention on occasion that he had thought about exhibiting himself. He felt he did not do it now because if he

93

did he would have to tell me, and that would make him unbearably ashamed. Incidentally, this attitude also reveals why it seems to me that it is unnecessary for the therapist to take an aggressive stand against the patient's symptom of sexual deviation (as sometimes advocated). Focusing on this particular case, it was obvious to the patient that this was a potentially self-destructive activity. In our relationship, it was taken for granted that we both knew this. My therapeutic orientation consisted of trying to help him to help himself in his own struggle with his symptom. If the therapist takes a more active stand against the symptom (with an analyzable patient), it seems to me that he encourages certain complications with which it may be extremely difficult to cope later on. Most important among these is the inference which the patient will draw, or which may even be stated explicitly by the therapist—namely, that the therapeutic relationship will be endangered, or will be discontinued, if the patient "disobeys" the therapist. This, I think, tends to make the patient even more phobic about his "impulses" than he already is, and makes facing his appropriate internal objects, and coming to terms with them, increasingly difficult and usually impossible. Symptom-cure may, of course, still be achieved, but it will probably rest on phobic avoidance mechanisms and on unconscious identifications with the therapist as an aggressive-benevolent "parent."

The full details of the circumstances which led up to the exhibitionistic act for which he was arrested emerged only gradually. Much of what follows is a condensation of all that was learned about this symptom during the entire course of the treatment. No attempt will be made to reconstruct the sequence in which various meanings of the exhibitionism emerged since I do not have the records which would be required for this task. Yet I must note that a sequential portrayal of these events would be very helpful for understanding the therapeutic process.

Exhibitionism is, of course, intimately connected with masturbation.

It is generally assumed in psychiatric texts that by exhibitionism it is meant that the patient exhibits his penis and that he masturbates at the same time. The further assumption is that the patient gains consciously pleasurable feelings from his "perverted" behavior. Yet, from all that I could learn from "K.," he never felt anything that he could describe as "sexual pleasure" (or any other pleasure) from exhibiting himself. Rather, his conscious experience was that he was under some sort of compulsion to act in this way, and following his overt exhibitionistic acts he would feel relieved of this need. Neither the need nor its satisfaction could, however, be referred to any bodily part. In this regard, as well as in many other of its features, the exhibitionistic behavior bore certain resemblances to patterns of counterphobic mastery, such as are evident in some sports, or in addictions. In simple terms, the crux of the matter seems to be that the patient carries out some bit of behavior that is dangerous, or which is forbidden, and he gains some satisfaction from thus proving both his independence (from whomever it may be) and his success in facing and surviving a dangerous situation.

Most of "K.'s" exhibitionistic behavior was of the following sort. He would lie in bed in the morning and would feign sleep while a woman, usually a maid, would try to tidy up his room. He would then uncover himself and handle his penis. He never ejaculated or experienced sexual arousal or orgasm. The exhibitionistic behavior seemed to be rather a gesture, that is to say, a communication achieved not through the use of words but by means of a body part and its movement. Certain phases of the treatment were chiefly concerned with attempts to make the necessary and correct translations from this gestural idiom to the language of every day English. What was he communicating and to whom by these "abortive" exhibitionistic movements in bed? "K." himself, of course, had never really tried to "understand" this behavior. He took it for granted that it existed and that it was terribly evil, but he tried to think as little as possible about it. He regarded it as a dreadful secret, perhaps like a contemporary American intellectual might regard his past affiliation with a subversive group. The dreaded "thing" was himself, or a part of himself, and yet he felt it was not. He feared, most of all, that "it" would be discovered. It was important to learn, in this connection, that his actual state of mind during exhibitionism was a peculiar one. He was not fully conscious in the sense of his own "normal" waking consciousness. He felt as if he were half asleep, or sometimes he felt de- realized or depersonalized. In other words he felt in part like an automaton which was exhibiting its penis, and all the while another part of him, completely devoid of feeling, was sitting somewhere outside watching what the automaton was doing. Needless to say, all this became clear to "K." only gradually, and only as he made his own exhibitionistic behavior an object of observation and study. He had never before done this, nor indeed had it even occurred to him that such a thing could be done.

By feigning sleep while exhibiting himself, he protected himself against the danger of being apprehended. If the cleaning woman did see him, she would think that he was asleep. Hence there would be no untoward consequences. He was further "insured," so to speak, by the uncertainty of whether or not he would be seen. Since he kept his eyes closed most of the time, he did not know if the woman looked in his direction. Actually, at the end of each of these episodes — which occurred quite infrequently, perhaps a few times a year — he never actually knew if he had been seen exhibiting himself or not. On rare occasions he had exhibited himself in a more direct manner, but always with considerable precautions against being apprehended. The episode that lead to his arrest was entirely at variance with his customary exhibitionism. Although the full details must be omitted, it can be stated that it was far more direct; so much so, in fact, that it was practically certain that the woman involved (whom he did not know personally) would summon others with the result that he would be apprehended. It was thus, in part, a gesture to invite arrest.

The circumstances which lead to his arrest were briefly these. "K." became involved with a marriageable young woman toward whom he felt his mother was pushing him. This, too, was a repetitive pattern. His mother would "find" girls for him—which he would let her do, although he inwardly objected to it—and he would "go out" with them but try to arrange things so that they would lose interest in him. And all the while he tried to conduct himself in such a way as to not "offend" anyone, especially his mother. It was unthinkable that he should refuse to go out with these girls. After all, he felt, his mother had proved to him that these were "nice girls" and good potential wives. What argument could he have against this? He literally became rooted to the "logic" of his mother's argument and ignored the "logic" of the total situation, and particularly his relationship to his mother. A situation now arose in which he believed his entanglement with a woman was getting out of hand. She was interested in him and for her own personal reasons was desperately eager to get married. This threw "K." into a panic. How was he to extricate himself? What could he tell his mother? What should he say to this woman? There seemed to be no way out — for he was confronted now with the one situation he was least able to handle, namely, to assert himself openly, verbally, vis-a-vis an important woman! The difficulty was, indeed, doubled, for he was confronted by two women who demanded that he do something which he felt he could not do. He felt powerless. Yet to pursue further the relationship with this woman seemed out of the question. He thought that it was certain to lead to marriage, and this was unthinkable. Just before his next date with her he exhibited himself in such a way that he was arrested. He immediately felt relieved from the mounting panic about being pushed into marriage. His arrest would have to be made known to his parents. This, of course, would mean that he would not be able to associate further with this woman. He could break with her, deliberately and definitely, once he convinced himself, by his arrest, that he was a "sexual pervert," a "dirty" and unworthy person. Thus he was not "refusing" her something that she wanted, but rather was "protecting" her. This turn of events also made it possible for "K." to promptly seek and begin analytic treatment, something which he had long desired. This, too, he felt he could undertake now without antagonizing, or implicitly criticizing, his parents.

Exhibitionism as a Communication

Certain communicative implications or meanings of his exhibitionism were brought to the fore in the very first interview. Having related that he had "exhibited himself" (I did not know exactly what he meant by this), and that he had been arrested, he added that of course he would now be forced to tell his parents about this. It was evident that at least one part of him—the part that felt "good" and "clean"— did not want to do this. In accordance with his conscious wishes he had kept everything concerning his sexual life a secret from his parents until this time. It did not seem to me that there was any obvious reason to communicate to them now anything which caused him to feel ashamed, any more than there had been before, and I told him so. He was taken aback by this. It did not seem possible to him not to tell them about this catastrophe. It is important to note that while "K." was generally able to entertain multiple possibilities and have rational doubts about various courses of action, in this instance only one course of action seemed open to him. And that was to tell his parents what happened. His feeling about breaking off with the woman whom his mother wanted him to marry was similarly single-minded. That is to say, it had not occurred to him that he might still marry her. This, of course, immediately suggested that the sexual act (and probably the arrest, as well) had been intended, in part, as a communication to his parents, particularly his mother. Ample evidence appeared later to support this assumption, and I shall present it shortly. Before doing so, however, I must note here that raising the question of the necessity for communicating with his parents, which I did in the first hour, proved to be quite a significant event. As it happened, he never again communicated anything he regarded as shameful to them, a behavior pattern in which he had engaged and for which he "hated himself." Calling his attention to this proved to be significant for two interrelated reasons. First, it made him aware that he did not wish to shame himself before them but that he felt this was expected of him. Second, it made him aware of an internal struggle between feelings of "badness" and unworthiness on the one hand, and a self-image of, and striving for, "goodness" and decency on the other hand. By not communicating with his parents, he felt later on, he saved himself another actual event that he would have listed on the debit side of his character.

Numerous facets of the communicative meanings of his exhibitionism were touched on in the course of the treatment. In a general way, the dominant meaning and determinant of this act was that it was a covert sign of rebellion against — and self-assertion from — his parents. He regarded himself as imprisoned and viewed his parents as omnipresent wardens. During his adult years, when he lived in cities at a distance from his parents, "K." still felt "imprisoned" by them. They were now his internal objects and manifested their presence by constantly reminding him, by means of self- accusations and feelings of shame and guilt, that they stood over him, as they had done before, and that they continued to condemn him. This was the single most dominant theme of "K.'s" self-experience. I commented on this earlier when I remarked on the similarities between "K.'s" dominant self-experience and object relationships on the one hand, and those of "Joseph K.," the hero of two of Kafka's novels, on the other. Hence, the sub-title of my presentation: The Case of Prisoner "K."

I have already commented on some of the reasons why "K" developed such an intense feeling of being controlled by his parents. Determinants of his efforts to establish self-control (to "rebel") in the specific ways he did were as follows:

1. His mother's monomaniacal preoccupation with his masturbation, that is, his touching his penis. In exhibiting himself he did precisely what his mother most stringently prohibited. Hence it had the special symbolic value of signifying his independence from her. In terms of its deepest unconscious meanings, this symptom (exhibitionism) further signified killing his mother (and father). And his strong fears and defenses against exhibiting himself derived, in part, from his wish to protect himself against committing this symbolic homicide.

2. A curious event occurred at about the age of eight, when he was actually asked to "exhibit himself," so to speak. What happened was this: While playing with a little girl, he was "accidentally" kicked in the genital area by her. He experienced considerable pain and the adults in charge feared that he was injured. A female relative and the little girl's mother insisted that he show them "where it hurt," and this meant showing them his penis. He was extremely embarrassed and ashamed, but finally acceded. He did not know why he gave in. Perhaps because they persuaded him, or because he was afraid that he was hurt, or perhaps for other reasons. There was, however, no significant physical injury. After this experience he developed a secondary shame and embarrassment over having been embarrassed. He was told "It was all right" to show his genitals, hence, he told himself, he should not have felt embarrassed. The memory of this event, and of these affects, was quite fresh; he had never ceased thinking about it. I might add that "K." suffered from nocturnal enuresis until shortly after this incident.

3. His mother's interest—and to a lesser extent his father's too — in his sexual life was revealed clearly in their anxious preoccupation concerning his "sexual normality." At some point well along in his treatment, he recollected the experience of his first ejaculation at about the age of nine or. ten. He was masturbating, had an orgasm, and saw some milky fluid exuding from his penis. He felt scared and bewildered. He went into his parents' bedroom and told them that he

was awakened from a bad dream. He thereupon told his father — and indirectly his mother, who was also present — that he "dreamed" that he was urinating, but that instead of urine "something else" came out. His father "understood" the message correctly, that is, as it was intended, and told the little boy that it was all right and that they would talk about it in the morning. "K." did not remember whether they had talked about it again. What seemed to me especially significant in this incident was, first, that "K." framed his communication to his parents in the form of a dream, and second, that it was a clear expression of the need to "confess" his "bad sexuality" to them, The latter was an important feature of his exhibitionism. In this form he communicated and confessed his "bad sexuality" to his parents who were hidden, so to speak, in the anonymous woman to whom he exhibited himself. The communication was addressed to "himself" as well, for his parents continued to reside within him as internal objects.

Telling his parents that he had a dream, when in fact he did not, is an important phenomenon in itself, but I cannot explore its various psychological implications here. Note, however, that by doing this, he accomplished, at least two things. First, his communication about his sexual behavior was sufficiently indirect so as to assure himself that he could not be blamed for it. Second, he diluted his own sense of "badness" and guilt for what he felt was a reprehensible activity. Not only do others not blame us for what we do in our dreams, but we treat ourselves in a similar manner. This childhood dream-communication was re-enacted in all of its essential details in his habitual exhibitionism while simulating sleep. In his outward behavior, he created the impression that he was asleep; while in his inner experience, he felt depersonalized, that is to say, not "fully awake."

4. During his teens, "K.'s" mother told him how a man had once exhibited himself to her in the subway. As he grew older, she also made a point of commenting on the accounts of "sex crimes" in the

newspapers, adding that it would "kill her" if "K." ever did anything like that.

5. The exhibitionism was, in a sense, also a communication which originated in one part of himself and was directed to another. Its source was his feeling of doubt about his sexual identity. This is to say, was he "his mother" or "his father"? He wanted to be neither. Was he castrated? And so forth. Seeing and touching his penis at least defined his sexual identity and role as clearly "masculine." One of the meanings of the exhibitionism could thus be paraphrased as follows : "I am not a woman — I am not crazy like my mother."

Termination of the Treatment

In this presentation I have drifted, perhaps unavoidably, far afield in the course of setting forth many of the things which "K." and I discovered in talking with each other. I have said little concerning his "transference neurosis," in the sense of the development of many of the conflicts with me which he had with his parents. The reason for this is partly that "K.'s" relationship to me never became nearly as intense as it did to his parents. A more "full blown" transference neurosis develops with some of my patients. In this case, however, since "K." felt so intensely threatened by being controlled, much of his relationship to me remained on the level of his fears of a repetition of this sort of a situation in treatment. He had similar fears concerning marriage. Accordingly, it seemed to me that "K." wished most of all to become less fearful of human entanglements. This could be shown to him, in innumerable forms, in his defenses against the "transference," or more correctly, against trusting me to the point of relinquishing his vigilance for fear that I would misuse my power over him. In view of his personal history and situation, however, it seemed that for "K." this point would constitute precisely the state in which he would not need, and would have no further interest in, psychoanalytic treatment. All this we discussed. As his relationship to me became less guarded, he talked frankly and forthrightly, and displayed a psychologically penetrating attitude toward me and himself. At the same time, he longed to be "free" of me and of the treatment. After everything was said and done, he felt, the "therapy," and his very relationship to me signified to him that he had had the problem of "exhibitionism," and it, in turn, signified his "bad" parental objects from whom he wanted increasingly to free himself. His relationship to his parents and others underwent considerable changes. He continued to maintain a superficially friendly contact with his parents, but in reality had almost no relationship with them. And he felt increasingly free of them. He was comfortable with the thought that he would know how to cope with anything which might arise — trying to master in his imagination, for example, how he would conduct himself if his father were to die first, or if his mother died first, and so forth. His sexual behavior also became more comfortable and less "driven." He lost interest in prostitutes and masturbated occasionally with satisfaction and without apparent conflict. Masturbation had meant, among other things, that he had a right to his body, including his penis, and could do as he wanted with it. It was another facet of the all-important matter of "Who controls him?"—is it his mother or father, the analyst (as "real" external or as internal objects) — or himself? Last, but not least, with the extensive "mapping out" of his exhibitionism — its origin and its various meanings, old as well as recent — and the working through of his relationship with his parents and me, his interest in exhibiting himself disappeared. What gratified him even more, however, was that he did not have a fear of its recurrence. I mention this specifically because before treatment he could imagine that he would not exhibit himself as a result of therapy, but he could not imagine that he would not contemplate and fear its recurrence.

It was at this point in our relationship that the treatment was terminated. This came about primarily in response to his own inclination to discontinue treatment. He felt that he had learned enough about himself and others; and while he felt no interest in a serious relationship with a woman, he could comfortably contemplate such an occurrence and thought that some years hence he might wish to be married. Last, but not least, he felt free and enjoyed this feeling immensely. He read more widely, he enjoyed his daily activities more fully, and he was astonished at his freedom from feelings of "sinfulness," "dirtiness," and "badness," which had always plagued him so much. He felt like a decent human being. The main thing which now constrained him was the treatment. We discussed in detail the connection he made between "receiving psychotherapy" and "being sick or sexually abnormal," as if the former state would prove to him the existence of the latter. He willingly scrutinized these, and similar connections, but the wish to discontinue treatment remained unaltered. There was, simply, nothing more that he wanted from the treatment, or from his relationship with me. Last but not least, he was putting to a test — or so I thought — whether or not I meant to control him, as did his parents before me. In other words, it seemed as though he wanted to see whether he was "really free" in relation to me, and he could prove this in no better way than by ascertaining my reaction to his wish to discontinue the treatment. We discussed this, and also the underlying assumption which continued to linger on, namely that I was a "bad" (persecuting and controlling) object, much like his parents were to him, and that my helpfulness was merely a facade. He could see the relevance of these constructions and could even acknowledge feeling a certain apprehension in relation to me, stemming from the above-mentioned sources. Yet, the fact remained that he felt that, at this time, he could gain more by stopping the treatment than by continuing it. He also felt that my interpretations of his wishes to stop were designed to make him continue. The situation with which I was confronted was simply as if he had said: "Actions speak louder than words." The subject-matter about which he spoke, in terms of this proverbial metaphor, pertained to his self-determination: Could he, or could he not, decide to stop the treatment? He had started it under duress. He was now asking whether he should continue under duress or whether he was free, at least in relation to me. All this we discussed. And we agreed to stop the treatment. It was clear to him that if in the future he wished to learn more about himself and his relationship to people, he could— and would have to — initiate further therapy on his own volition.

Finally, at about this time, an opportunity arose for "K." to engage in an activity closely related to his work which strongly appealed to him. To avail himself of this opportunity, he had to move to another part of the country. He welcomed this turn of events, not only for the "primary" benefits which they afforded, but equally as much for the opportunity to separate himself still further (geographically) from his parents, and from me —and lastly also from the scene of his arrest, which remained, at least while I still saw him, a place where he did not want to live for the remainder of his life. I concurred with "K." that this was an opportune time for us to part. We had now been seeing each other four times a week for thirty months.

Conclusions: Nosology and Psychotherapy

"*Traditional language always seems clear. There seems to be great clarity in such sentences as these: Heat flows. Life left him. He is possessed of a devil. He has a disease. He has a neurosis. But, for all their apparent clarity, they are surely all wrong. Their categories are wrong. All of them assert false substantives, when the discussion should be couched in terms of processes.*" (G. Hardin)

Before concluding this account of my efforts to bring a psychoanalytic type of "influence" (a term which I prefer to that of "treatment") to bear on my patient, "K.," I would like to offer some brief comments on "K." as a person and on the treatment process which I described.

I have for some time now been firmly convinced that our contemporary systems of psychiatric nosology are worthless insofar as our interest is to understand the patient, and our aim is to help him by means of psychoanalytic treatment. This does not negate the usefulness of a so-called "psychiatric diagnosis" for other purposes, for instance for determining whether or not legal action should be taken toward someone who has violated the law. These two tasks, however, have practically nothing in common. They are combined so often only because the same persons (i.e. psychiatrists) have assumed social roles in both therapeutic and legal situations. In accordance with this view, I do not believe that there is such a thing as "psychopathology" independent of a social situation in which it is anchored and from which it derives the values of "normal" and "pathological." Hence, I would not offer any "diagnosis" to identify the "mental illness" from which "K." could be said to have suffered. Obviously enough, according to present day psychiatric usage, his "illness" would be labeled a "sexual perversion," sometimes more elegantly called a "sexual deviation." Or he might have been simply "diagnosed" as an "exhibitionist." Clearly, none of these designations tells us anything whatsoever about "K." as a human being, what troubled him, and what he was trying to do about it.

In regard to "K.'s" chief "symptom," the exhibitionism, I came to the conclusion on the basis of what I was able to learn from him that there was very little that could be said to have been "sexual" about this behavior, I hasten to add that by "sexual" I refer to an affect which is experienced as erotic feeling or which can become so by becoming conscious. In this sense of the word "sexual," exhibitionism proved to be, at least for "K." a form of non-sexual behavior and communication implemented by means of the (male) genital organ. The prevalent lay opinion as well as professional (i.e., medical and psychiatric) opinion which views this form of behavior as a "perversion," that is as a particular ("abnormal") form of sexual experience and sexual gratification stems from confusion in regard to what the experiencing person feels and what the observer of this behavior believes he feels. The manifest genitality of the behavior impresses the observer as a sign of sexual activity, and hence, by inference, as a sign of sexual experience (affect). This inference, while usually valid for many forms of sexual activity, is still an inference, and not an equivalence. "K.'s" exhibitionism was principally an expression of his struggle for "freedom" from his oppressive internal (and external) objects. He experienced his need to exhibit himself as a vague and unverbalized tension-state. It was definitely not a form of "sexual tension." The experiencing of sexual tension was an affective state, familiar to him, which he was prone to relieve by masturbation (without exhibitionism) and by sexual intercourse with prostitutes. Since my experience with "K.," several other cases have confirmed my impression that exhibitionism is a form of non-sexual behavior expressed by means of the genital organ. In none of these cases, however, did I know the patient as well as one knows a patient in analysis. In fact, I saw these other patients only for purposes of "diagnosis" during my period of service as a navy psychiatrist. None experienced erotic feelings during the act. And while all of them assumed—in conformity with the prevalent social view — that this was a "sexual deviation," when I asked them directly whether they felt that their exhibitionism was "sexual" they were all nonplussed. The act seemed to have been directed, in each case, toward one or another parent, and, in condensed form, expressed the patient's conflict with this oppressive object (his rebellion against the object, his statement of self-assertion from the object, and his submission to the object through guilt and/or apprehension). The communicative role and significance of this behavior was shown further, in "K.'s" case, by his speech impediment. So much for the psychology of "K.'s" exhibitionism.

Although I indicated my wish to avoid using any of the misleading diagnostic labels currently fashionable, it might be useful to think of "K." as having a "schizoid personality" (or "schizophrenic core"). By this I simply mean that he might be more prone to have a schizophrenic type of "breakdown" — given the proper circumstances for it — than would someone else who had had the good fortune to have better internal objects less controlling, less ambivalent than he had. At the same time, "K.'s" relatively objectless living-pattern, both at the beginning and at the end of this treatment, is something that the word "schizoid" conveys quite well. In this, it stands in contrast to what may be considered as "more healthy" (at least for purposes of having a warm human relationship, though not necessarily for purposes of being a good "worker" or effective political or religious leader)—namely, the ability and proclivity for making lasting commitments to a few significant persons. I mention "K.'s" schizoid personality organization only because it had a bearing on the nature of the therapeutic relationship which evolved between us. It was characterized, as I noted before, by a certain "distance" between us. Instead of an extensive "transference neurosis," his predominant "transference" lay in the fact that in his relationship to me he manifested and experienced the same fears and reservations concerning "getting involved" (in an oppressive situation) as he did in relation to other people. This excessive self-protection derived from his deep conviction that behind various human facades there lurked, in everyone, the sort of person that his parents were to him. He feared re-exposing himself to "bad" (persecuting and controlling) objects. And, of course, we discussed — and I think he was able to see — that he also perceived me in this light. Much of the "analysis of the transference" revolved around this theme. Properly speaking, however, this sort of work should be labeled "analysis of the defenses against the transference."

While I believe that this method of therapy was appropriate, even inevitable in this particular situation, I want to emphasize that I think it is important to differentiate this from other types of transference-analysis. In people whose schizoid disposition is slight, the analytic process tends to evolve in a somewhat different fashion. Briefly, following analysis of the defenses against the transference (against the fears of a power-dependent relationship, as with one's parents), there appear in the patient's relationship to the analyst, re-enactments of features of his earlier relationship to his parents. This second type of "transference" behavior, and its analysis, was by no means completely absent in my work with "K."; but it was fragmentary and tended to be limited to certain isolated occurrences. This was the reason why I stated at the beginning of this essay that I did not consider this case to be the story of a "typical" analysis. It illustrates, however, many of the things which I consider to be characteristic of the psychoanalytic treatment relationship and process.

ADDENDUM

1. Optimally, what criteria do you use for accepting or rejecting patients for psychotherapy?

I cannot answer this question in this form, since I believe that there are a very large (if not limitless) number of different psychotherapies. Different methods of selection would apply to each. (See in this connection my answer to question 11.) My answer, therefore, applies only to psychoanalysis, and in part perhaps only to a somewhat idealized version of it. My main criteria for accepting patients for analysis (the criteria for rejecting can be inferred from the degree to which the prospective patient fails to meet these criteria) are the following:

(a) The patient should seek therapy because of some disturbance which he feels is his; he should not consult the therapist solely because he is driven to him, in one form or another (as is frequently the case) by others, and he must not request to be analyzed for the sake of others. Instead, he should desire and hope to achieve a personal goal of his own.

(b) He should be at least of average intelligence, and should possess the interest and the ability to look at himself and at his relationships (past, present, and future) with people. He may not be able to do this for cultural, religious, and "psychopathological" reasons. These three categories which overlap are used here mainly descriptively. Illustrative considerations are the following. Does the person value action or contemplation? Does he favor religious group-identity or scientific solitude? And finally, does he tend toward "psychotic" certainty or is he comfortable with "normal-neurotic" doubt? I deliberately exaggerate and dichotomize certain psychological phenomena to make a point. The closer the patient approaches the first position in these paired characteristics, the less likely am I to accept him for psychoanalysis (or analytic psychotherapy).

(c) The patient should be as free as possible in his social and economic relationships. (According to this criterion, children are excluded - "by definition," so to speak — from being proper subjects for psychoanalysis. They may be excluded on other grounds as well.)

(d) Diagnostic considerations, in the sense of formal nosological entities, play virtually no part in my selection of patients for psychoanalytic psychotherapy. (See question 2 below.)

2. Do you make a diagnosis before psychotherapy begins?

I cannot answer this question without commenting on the word "diagnosis," which I consider to be seriously misleading if used in connection with psychotherapeutic considerations. In other words, if "diagnosis" refers to ascertaining the kind of "psychiatric disease"— such as hysteria, obsessive-compulsive neurosis, schizophrenia, and so forth — the patient "has" — then my answer would be that I do not make a "diagnosis" before beginning psychotherapy. If, however, "diagnosis" refers to gaining an impression of the sort of person the patient is, how he grew up, the nature of his personal relationships and his work, the degree of his freedom in the conduct of his life, and so on (see question 1) — then I would answer emphatically "Yes!" I do make a "diagnosis."

3. Do you attempt to persuade the patient or significant relative to change his {the patient's) environment?

No. I refrain from such measures if I expect to conduct any kind of psychotherapy (including psychoanalysis) designed to help the patient to learn more about himself. The avoidance of this and other types of direct influence rests on the premise that if the patient learns more about himself and his human relationships he will be in a position to make his own decisions. If learning on the part of the patient is not considered to be the primary goal and function of the psychotherapy, then I would regard giving advice as appropriate.

4. How did you conceptualize the therapist's role in this case?

My concept of the therapist's role in this case was that of a particular form of the "analytic role." By this I refer to a distinctive human relationship (the analytic situation), and in it to the analyst's endeavor to. assist his patient solely by means of interpretive communications. (See question 3 above.)

5. What aspects of your theory of psychotherapy were particularly apparent or useful in the case presented here?

I think my thesis that psychoanalytic psychotherapy is a form of learning for the patient is apparent in this case. Specifically, the patient learns what sort of a person he is, and how he became what he is. This occurs in and through the analytic relationship, and usually enables the patient to use this relationship (and others) to modify his internal object-world, and hence "himself." To assist in making such self-transformation possible is one of the distinctive functions, in my opinion, of the work of the analyst.

6. Do you feel that this case developed significant insight? If not, can improvement he maintained?

For the sake of brevity, I want to say simply "Yes, I think this patient developed insight." (See question 5 above.) But to speak of "insight" without specifying "into what?" is to invite ambiguity.

7. What aspects of your own cultural orientation facilitated or impeded the treatment of your case?

I do not think that any particular orientation, beyond that implicit in psychoanalysis itself, played a significant part in the conduct of this treatment. Any method of psychotherapy which undertakes an inquiry into this patient's (and less explicitly into the therapist's) personal relationships, history, values, and so forth, rests on the premise that increased information and knowledge are positive values. This, in turn, rests on the further premise that the person is motivated by the hope of achieving mastery of his problems in relation to internal and external objects with the aid of increasingly complex psychological operations. The values implicit in psychoanalysis — at least as I see them — are thus in covert (sometimes direct) conflict with certain cultural and religious values; specifically, the two are in conflict whenever the latter explicitly declare that certain parts of "reality" must not be made the objects of skeptical inquiry (as some religious and political systems do). Such prohibitions recreate in adult life? the various prohibitions which are generally imposed upon children in most civilized societies. In some families, there is a specific prohibition against scrutinizing the parents' activities. This was of particular importance in the case which I presented. Similar prohibitions in the therapeutic situation, particularly on curiosities and doubts concerning the therapist, would tend to recreate the patient's original (childhood) "pathogenic" environment in his adult life.

8. If we consider that a continuum exists from superficial to deep psychotherapy, where would you place your own case?

I do not find the words "superficial" and "deep" in connection with psychotherapy at all useful. It seems to me that these words are used only as value judgments of the therapy to which they are applied. Thus, "superficial" seems to mean "poor" (or make-shift) and "deep" means "good" or "very effective." The distinction rests on, and embodies, the medical model of psychotherapy with "superficial" standing in the same relationship to "deep" as, say, aspirin stands in relation to penicillin in the treatment of pneumonia. This model is misleading. Accordingly, I would not rate my case in these terms.

9. What did you think about the outcome of this case and what criteria did you use for evaluating such outcome?

I consider the outcome of this case as satisfactory. My criteria for evaluating the outcome of therapy are multiple and range from the simplest and most concrete (for example, symptom change) all the way to the most abstract and difficult to assess (for example, estimation of what the patient has "learned" about himself and significant others). In this case, there was of course an important change ("improvement") in the chief symptoms (exhibitionism and stuttering). In addition, there were extensive changes in the patient's internal object-world, and concomitantly, there occurred major changes in his relationship to significant external objects (mostly his parents). Last but not least, he appeared to have been able to successfully understand and master some aspects of his relationship to me.

10. How do you terminate psychotherapy?

I generally adhere to two principles in regard to terminating psychotherapy. The first principle is that I allow the patient complete freedom to discontinue therapy whenever he wishes. The second principle is more general than the first and consists of making the termination of the therapy itself the object of analytic scrutiny. I thus try to make this a collaborative decision to be arrived at preferably only after extensive considerations of both the advantages and disadvantages that may result from continuing or stopping the treatment. Once I have accepted a patient for psychotherapy, I rarely, if ever, stop treatment as long as the patient wants to continue. If I think continuation is undesirable, I communicate this to the patient, stating my reasons for this recommendation. This has been an infrequent occurrence in my experience, but whenever it has occurred this procedure has proven to be satisfactory. The difficulties often mentioned by contemporary analysts in regard to "weaning" the patient away from analysis (or his allegedly "excessive dependence" upon the analyst) seems to me to stem directly from an unnecessarily authoritative feature of many analytic arrangements. I refer to the fact that it is understood, either overtly or sometimes by hidden innuendo, that the patient must not stop the analysis once he has started it without the express consent of the analyst, and preferably only at the latter's suggestion. Thus the patient is made to step from the relative freedom of his pre-analytic state, in which he was at least "free" to decide whether or not he wished to pursue analysis, into what must seem to him as an "analytic bondage." He often adapts to this by the well known maneuver of turning passivity into activity: "If I have to stay, I want to stay ..." I think it is desirable that the patient should have at least as much freedom in regard to his therapeutic relationship as he had when he (and the therapist) chose to initiate it. If psychotherapy is at all successful, the patient will only be in a better position (than he had been before) to decide for himself with the assistance of the therapist how long therapy will be profitable to him. And lastly, in case of a serious difference of opinion between patient and therapist about whether or not to stop, it seems to me incompatible with the psychological structure and philosophy of psychoanalysis (and psychoanalytic psychotherapy) for the therapist to try to arrogate to himself the role of making such an important decision as this for his patient.

11. Other.

I wish to call attention to what I consider to be a matter of paramount importance in connection with considerations of psychotherapy. It is that the word "psychotherapy" denotes a global type of concept and an almost infinite variety of actual therapeutic operations. In this regard, it is comparable to words such as "medicine," "mathematics," or "democracy." If we should ask what these things are, our answers could not be sought in simple definitions, nor even in extensive descriptions and illustrations. Instead, meaningful answers to such questions can only be found by studying and becoming familiar with entire scientific disciplines. This is — and must be — as true for psychotherapy as it is for medicine, mathematics, or political history and sociology. The methods of psychotherapy range all the way from hypnosis, giving advice, and "brain-washing" to various highly "democratic" (or equalitarian) forms of patient-therapist collaboration; and even within these collaborative methods, huge differences between different forms of psychological influencing exist, depending upon both the theoretical-scientific grasp of the participants concerning psychological happenings and upon the types of influence which they bring to bear on each other. To think, in the face of these differences, that "psychotherapy" possesses some fundamental unifying features (other, that is, than its obvious difference from physical methods of intervention) is nothing short of indulging in wishful thinking. Its net result is the codification of "psychotherapy" as a naively simplified and concretized "method" — a conception which only hinders progress toward the appreciation of the specific features of individual techniques. I visualize the collection of essays assembled in this volume as a contribution to this important goal.

6. PSYCHOTHERAPY AS A LEARNING PROCESS

(Albert Bandura 1961)

Classic paper by eminent psychologist Albert Bandura exploring systematic attempts to apply principles of learning to the area of psychotherapy. Bandura begins this exploration by asking whether human behavior can be modified through psychological means and if so, what are the learning mechanisms that mediate behavior change? He then sets about discussing some of these learning mechanisms in turn i.e., counterconditioning, extinction, discrimination learning, methods of reward, punishment and social imitation.

While it is customary to conceptualize psychotherapy as a learning process, few therapists accept the full implications of this position. Indeed, this is best illustrated by the writings of the learning theorists themselves. Most of our current methods of psychotherapy represent an accumulation of more or less uncontrolled clinical experiences and, in many instances, those who have written about psychotherapy in terms of learning theory have merely substituted a new language; the practice remains essentially unchanged(Dollard, Auld, & White, 1954; Dollard & Miller, 1950; Shoben, 1949).

One seriously subscribes to the view that psychotherapy is a learning process, the methods of treatment should be derived from our knowledge of learning and motivation. Such an orientation is likely to yield new techniques of treatment which, in many respects, may differ markedly from the procedures currently in use.

Psychotherapy rests on a very simple but fundamental assumption, i.e., human behavior is modifiable through psychological procedures. When skeptics raise the question, "Does psychotherapy work?" they may be responding in part to the mysticism that has come to surround the term. Perhaps the more meaningful question, and one which avoids the surplus meanings associated with the term "psychotherapy," is as follows: Can human behavior be modified through psychological means and if so, what are the learning mechanisms that mediate behavior change?

In the sections that follow, some of these learning mechanisms will be discussed, and studies in which systematic attempts have been made to apply these principles of learning to the area of psychotherapy will be reviewed. Since learning theory itself is still somewhat incomplete, the list of psychological processes by which changes in behavior can occur should not be regarded as exhaustive, nor are they necessarily without overlap.

COUNTERCONDITIONING

Of the various treatment methods derived from learning theory, those based on the principle of counterconditioning have been elaborated in greatest detail. Wolpe (1954, 1958, 1959) gives a thorough account of this method, and additional examples of cases treated in this manner are provided by Jones (1956), Lazarus and Rachman (1957), Meyer (1957), and Rachman (1959). Briefly, the principle involved is as follows: if strong responses which are incompatible with anxiety reactions can be made to occur in the presence of anxiety evoking cues, the incompatible responses will become attached to these cues and thereby weaken or eliminate the anxiety responses.

The first systematic psychotherapeutic application of this method was reported by Jones (1924b) in the treatment of Peter, a boy who showed severe phobic reactions to animals, fur objects, cotton, hair, and mechanical toys. Counterconditioning was achieved by feeding the child in the presence of initially small but gradually increasing anxiety-arousing stimuli. A rabbit in a cage was placed in the room at some distance so as not to disturb the boy's eating. Each day the rabbit was brought nearer to the table and eventually removed from the cage. During the final stage of treatment, the rabbit was placed on the feeding table and even in Peter's lap. Tests of generalization revealed that the fear responses had been effectively eliminated, not only toward the rabbit, but toward the previously feared furry objects as well.

In this connection, it would be interesting to speculate on the diagnosis and treatment Peter would have received had he been seen by Melanie Klein (1949) rather than by Mary Cover Jones!

It is interesting to note that while both Shoben (1949) and Wolpe (1958) propose a therapy based on the principle of counterconditioning, their treatment methods are radically different. According to Shoben, the patient discusses and thinks about stimulus situations that are anxiety provoking in the context of an interpersonal situation which simultaneously elicits positive affective responses from the patient. The therapeutic process consists in connecting the anxiety provoking stimuli, which are symbolically reproduced, with the comfort reaction made to the therapeutic relationship.

Shoben's paper represents primarily a counterconditioning interpretation of the behavior changes brought about through conventional forms of psychotherapy since, apart from highlighting the role of positive emotional reactions in the treatment process, no new techniques deliberately designed to facilitate relearning through counterconditioning are proposed.

This is not the case with Wolpe, who has made a radical departure from tradition. In his treatment, which he calls reciprocal inhibition, Wolpe makes systematic use of three types of responses which are antagonistic to, and therefore inhibitory of, anxiety. These are:

assertive or approach responses, sexual responses, and relaxation responses.

On the basis of historical information, interview data, and psychological test responses, the therapist constructs an anxiety hierarchy, a ranked list of stimuli to which the patient reacts with anxiety. In the case of desensitization based on relaxation, the patient is hypnotized and given relaxation suggestions. He is then asked to imagine a scene representing the weakest item on the anxiety hierarchy and, if the relaxation is unimpaired, this is followed by having the patient imagine the next item on the list, and so on. Thus, the anxiety cues are gradually increased from session to session until the last phobic stimulus can be presented without impairing the relaxed state. Through this procedure, relaxation responses eventually come to be attached to the anxiety evoking stimuli.

Wolpe reports remarkable therapeutic success with a wide range of neurotic reactions treated on this counterconditioning principle. He also contends that the favorable outcomes achieved by the more conventional psychotherapeutic methods may result from the reciprocal inhibition of anxiety by strong positive responses evoked in the patient-therapist relationship.

Although the counterconditioning method has been employed most extensively in eliminating anxiety motivated avoidance reactions and inhibitions, it has been used with some success in reducing maladaptive approach responses as well. In the latter case, the goal object is repeatedly associated with some form of aversive stimulus.

Raymond (1956), for example, used nausea as the aversion experience in the treatment of a patient who presented a fetish for handbags and perambulators which brought him into frequent contact with the law in that he repeatedly smeared mucus on ladies' handbags and destroyed perambulators by running into them with his motorcycle. Though the patient had undergone psychoanalytic treatment, and was fully aware of the origin and the sexual significance of his behavior, nevertheless, the fetish persisted.

The treatment consisted of showing the patient a collection of handbags, perambulators, and colored illustrations just before the onset of nausea produced by injections of apomorphine. The conditioning was repeated every 2 hours day and night for 1 week plus additional sessions 8 days and 6 months later.

Raymond reports that, not only was the fetish successfully eliminated, but also the patient showed a vast improvement in his social (and legal) relationships, was promoted to a more responsible position in his work, and no longer required the fetish fantasies to enable him to have sexual intercourse.

Nauseant drugs, especially emetine, have also been utilized as the unconditioned stimulus in the aversion treatment of alcoholism (Thirmann, 1949; Thompson & Bielinski, 1953; Voegtlen, 1940; Wallace, 1949). Usually 8 to 10 treatments in which the sight, smell, and taste of alcohol is associated with the onset of nausea is sufficient to produce abstinence. Of 1,000 or more cases on whom adequate follow-up data are reported, approximately 60% of the patients have been totally abstinent following the treatment. Voegtlen (1940) suggests that a few preventive treatments given at an interval of about 6 months may further improve the results yielded by this method.

Despite these encouraging findings, most psychotherapists are unlikely, to be impressed since, in their opinion, the underlying causes for the alcoholism have in no way been modified by the conditioning procedure and, if anything, the mere removal of the alcoholism would tend to produce symptom substitution or other adverse effects. A full discussion of this issue will be presented later.

In this particular context, however, several aspects of the Thompson and Bielinski (1953) data are worth noting. Among the alcoholic patients whom they treated, six "suffered from mental disorders not due to alcohol or associated deficiency states." It was planned, by the authors, to follow up the aversion treatment with psychotherapy for the underlying psychosis. This, however, proved unnecessary since all but one of the patients, a case of chronic mental deterioration, showed marked improvement and were in a state of remission.

Max (1935) employed a strong electric shock as the aversive stimulus in treating a patient who tended to display homosexual behavior following exposure to a fetishistic stimulus. Both the fetish and the homosexual behavior were removed through a series of avoidance conditioning sessions in which the patient was administered shock in the presence of the fetishistic object.

Wolpe (1958) has also reported favorable results with a similar procedure in the treatment of obsessions. A further variation of the counterconditioning procedure has been developed by Mowrer and Mowrer (1938) for use with enuretic patients. The device consists of a wired bed pad which sets off a loud buzzer and awakens the child as soon as micturition begins. Bladder tension thus becomes a cue for waking up which, in turn, is followed by sphincter contraction. Once bladder pressure becomes a stimulus for the more remote sphincter control response, the child is able to remain dry for relatively long periods of time without wakening.

Mowrer and Mowrer (1938) report complete success with 30 children treated by this method; similarly, Davidson and Douglass (1950) achieved highly successful results with 20 chronic enuretic children (15 cured, 5 markedly improved); of 5 cases treated by Morgan and Witmer (1939), 4 of the children not only gained full sphincter control, but also made a significant improvement in their social behavior. The one child with whom the conditioning approach had failed was later found to have bladder difficulties which required medical attention.

Some additional evidence for the efficacy of this method is provided by Martin and Kubly (1955) who obtained follow-up information from 118 of 220 parents who had treated their children at home with this type of conditioning apparatus. In 74% of the cases, according to the parents' replies, the treatment was successful.

EXTINCTION

"When a learned response is repeated without reinforcement the strength of the tendency to perform that response undergoes a progressive decrease" (Dollard & Miller, 1950). Extinction involves the development of inhibitory potential which is composed of two components. The evocation of any reaction generates reactive inhibition which presumably dissipates with time. When reactive inhibition (fatigue, etc.) reaches a high point, the cessation of activity alleviates this negative motivational state and any stimuli associated with the cessation of the response become conditioned inhibitors.

One factor that has been shown to influence the rate of extinction of maladaptive and anxiety-motivated behavior is the interval between extinction trials. In general, there tends to be little diminution in the strength of fear-motivated behavior when extinction trials are widely distributed, whereas under massed trials, reactive inhibition builds up rapidly and consequently extinction is accelerated (Calvin, Clifford, Clifford, Bolden, & Harvey, 1956; Edmonson & Amsel, 1954).

An illustration of the application of this principle is provided by Yates (1958) in the treatment of tics. Yates demonstrated, in line with the findings from laboratory studies of extinction under massed and distributed practice, that massed sessions in which the patient performed tics voluntarily followed by prolonged rest to allow for the dissipation of reactive inhibition was the most effective procedure for extinguishing the tics.

It should be noted that the extinction procedure employed by Yates is very similar to Dunlap's method of negative practice, in which the subject reproduces the negative behaviors voluntarily without reinforcement (Dunlap, 1932; Lehner, 1954). This method has been applied most frequently, with varying degrees of success, to the treatment of speech disorders (Fishman, 1937; Meissner, 1946; Rutherford, 1940; Sheehan, 1951; Sheehan & Voas, 1957). If the effectiveness of this psychotherapeutic technique is due primarily to extinction, as suggested by Yates study, the usual practice of terminating a treatment session before the subject becomes fatigued (Lehner, 1954), would have the effect of reducing the rate of extinction, and may in part account for the divergent results yielded by this method.

Additional examples of the therapeutic application of extinction procedures are provided by Jones (1955), and most recently by C. D. Williams (1959).

Most of the conventional forms of psychotherapy rely heavily on extinction effects although the therapist may not label these as such. For example, many therapists consider permissiveness to be a necessary condition of therapeutic change (Alexander, 1956; Dollard & Miller, 1950; Rogers, 1951). It is expected that when a patient expresses thoughts or feelings that provoke anxiety or guilt and the therapist does not disapprove, criticize, or withdraw interest, the fear or guilt will be gradually weakened or extinguished. The extinction effects are believed to generalize to thoughts concerning related topics that were originally inhibited, and to verbal and physical forms of behavior as well (Dollard & Miller, 1950).

Some evidence for the relationship between permissiveness and the extinction of anxiety is provided in two studies recently reported by Dittes (1957a, 1957b). In one study (1957b) involving an analysis of patient therapist interaction sequences, Dittes found that permissive responses on the part of the therapist were followed by a corresponding decrease in the patient's anxiety (as measured by the GSR) and the occurrence of avoidance behaviors. A sequential analysis of the therapeutic sessions (Dittes, 1957a), revealed that, at the onset of treatment, sex expressions were accompanied by strong anxiety reactions; under the cumulative effects of permissiveness, the anxiety gradually extinguished.

In contrast to counterconditioning, extinction is likely to be a less effective and a more time consuming method for eliminating maladaptive behavior (Jones, 1924a; Dollard & Miller, 1950); in the case of conventional interview therapy, the relatively long intervals between interview sessions, and the ritualistic adherence to the 50-minute hour may further reduce the occurrence of extinction effects.

DISCRIMINATION LEARNING

Human functioning would be extremely difficult and inefficient if a person had to learn appropriate behavior for every specific situation he encountered. Fortunately, patterns of behavior learned in one situation will transfer or generalize to other similar situations. On the other hand, if a person over generalizes from one situation to another, or if the generalization is based on superficial or irrelevant cues, behavior becomes inappropriate and maladaptive.

In most theories of psychotherapy, therefore, discrimination learning, believed to be accomplished through the gaining of awareness or insight, receives emphasis (Dollard & Miller, 1950; Fenichel, 1941; Rogers, 1951; Sullivan, 1953). It is generally assumed that if a patient is aware of the cues producing his behavior, of the responses he is making, and of the reasons that he responds the way he does, his behavior will become more susceptible to verbally-mediated control. Voluntarily guided, discriminative behavior will replace the automatic, over generalized reactions.

While this view is widely accepted, as evidenced in the almost exclusive reliance on interview procedures and on interpretative or labeling techniques, a few therapists (Alexander & French, 1946) have questioned the importance attached to awareness in producing modifications in behavior. Whereas most psychoanalysts (Fenichel, 1941), as well as therapists representing other points of view (Fromm-Reichmann, 1950; Sullivan, 1953) consider insight a precondition of behavior change, Alexander and French consider insight or awareness a result of change rather than its cause. That is, as the patient's anxieties are gradually reduced through the permissive conditions of treatment, formerly inhibited thoughts are gradually restored to awareness.

Evidence obtained through controlled laboratory studies concerning the value of awareness in increasing the precision of discrimination has so far been largely negative or at least equivocal (Adams, 1957; Erikson, 1958; Razran, 1949). A study by Lacy and Smith (1954), in which they found aware subjects generalized anxiety reactions less extensively than did subjects who were unaware of the conditioned stimulus provides evidence that awareness may aid discrimination. However, other aspects of their findings (e.g., the magnitude of the anxiety reactions to the generalization stimuli were greater than they were to the conditioned stimulus itself) indicate the need for replication.

If future research continues to demonstrate that awareness exerts little influence on the acquisition, generalization, and modification of behavior, such negative results would cast serious doubt on the value of currently popular psychotherapeutic procedures whose primary aim is the development of insight.

METHODS OF REWARD

Most theories of psychotherapy are based on the assumption that the patient has a repertoire of previously learned positive habits available to him, but that these adaptive patterns are inhibited or blocked by competing responses motivated by anxiety or guilt. The goal of therapy, then, is to reduce the severity of the internal inhibitory controls, thus allowing the healthy patterns of behavior to emerge. Hence, the role of the therapist is to create permissive conditions under which the patient's "normal growth potentialities" are set free (Rogers, 1951). The fact that most of our theories of personality and therapeutic procedures have been developed primarily through work with over socialized, neurotic patients may account in part for the prevalence of this view. There is a large class of disorders (the under socialized, antisocial personalities whose behavior reflects a failure of the socialization process) for whom this model of personality and accompanying techniques of treatment are quite inappropriate (Bandura & Walters, 1959; Schmideberg, 1959). Such antisocial personalities are likely to present learning deficits, consequently the goal of therapy is the acquisition of secondary motives and the development of internal restraint habits. That antisocial patients prove unresponsive to psychotherapeutic methods developed for the treatment of over socialized neurotics has been demonstrated in a number of studies comparing patients who remain in treatment with those who terminate treatment prematurely (Rubenstein & Lorr, 1956). It is for this class of patients that the greatest departures from traditional treatment methods is needed.

While counterconditioning, extinction, and discrimination learning may be effective ways of removing neurotic inhibitions, these methods may be of relatively little value in developing new positive habits. Primary and secondary rewards in the form of the therapist's interest and approval may play an important, if not indispensable, role in the treatment process. Once the patient has learned to want the interest and approval of the therapist, these rewards may then be used to promote the acquisition of new patterns of behavior. For certain classes of patients such as schizophrenics (Atkinson, 1957; Peters, 1953; Robinson, 1957) and delinquents (Cairns, 1959), who are either unresponsive to, or fearful of, social rewards, the therapist may have to rely initially on primary rewards in the treatment process.

An ingenious study by Peters and Jenkins (1954) illustrates the application of this principle in the treatment of schizophrenic patients. Chronic patients from closed wards were administered sub shock injections of insulin designed to induce the hunger drive. The patients were then encouraged to solve a series of graded problem tasks with fudge as the reward. This program was followed 5 days a week for 3 months.

Initially the tasks involved simple mazes and obstruction problems in which the patients obtained the food reward directly upon successful completion of the problem. Tasks of gradually increasing difficulty were then administered involving multiple-choice learning and verbal-reasoning problems in which the experimenter personally mediated the primary rewards. After several weeks of such problem solving activities the insulin injections were discontinued and social rewards, which by this time had become more effective, were used in solving interpersonal problems that the patients were likely to encounter in their daily activities both inside and outside the hospital setting.

Comparison of the treated group with control groups, designed to isolate the effects of insulin and special attention, revealed that the patients in the reward group improved significantly in their social relationships in the hospital, whereas the patients in the control groups showed no such change.

King and Armitage (1958) report a somewhat similar study in which severely withdrawn schizophrenic patients were treated with operant conditioning methods; candy and cigarettes served as the primary rewards for eliciting and maintaining increasingly complex forms of behavior, i.e., psychomotor, verbal, and interpersonal responses. Unlike the Peters and Jenkins study, no attempt was made to manipulate the level of primary motivation.

An interesting feature of the experimental design was the inclusion of a group of patients who were treated with conventional interview therapy, as well as a recreational therapy and a no-therapy control group. It was found that the operant group, in relation to similar patients in the three control groups, made significantly more clinical improvement.

Skinner (1956b) and Lindsley (1956) working with adult psychotics, and Ferster (1959) working with autistic children, have been successful in developing substantial amounts of reality-oriented behavior in their patients through the use of reward. So far their work has been concerned primarily with the effect of schedules of reinforcement on the rate of evocation of simple impersonal reactions. There is every indication, however, that by varying the contingency of the reward (e.g., the patient must respond in certain specified ways to the behavior of another individual in order to produce the reward) adaptive interpersonal behaviors can be developed as well (Azran & Lindsley, 1956).

The effectiveness of social reinforcers in modifying behavior has been demonstrated repeatedly in verbal conditioning experiments (Krasner, 1958; Salzinger, 1959). Encouraged by these findings, several therapists have begun to experiment with operant conditioning as a method of treatment in its own right (Tilton, 1956; Ullman, Krasner, & Collins, in press; R. I. Williams, 1959); the operant conditioning studies cited earlier are also illustrative of this trend.

So far the study of generalization and permanence of behavior changes brought about through operant conditioning methods has received relatively little attention and the scanty data available are equivocal (Rogers, 1960; Sarason, 1957; Weide, 1959). The lack of consistency in results is hardly surprising considering that the experimental manipulations in many of the conditioning studies are barely sufficient to demonstrate conditioning effects, let alone generalization of changes to new situations. On the other hand, investigators who have conducted more intensive reinforcement sessions, in an effort to test the efficacy of operant conditioning methods as a therapeutic technique, have found significant changes in patients' interpersonal behavior in extra-experimental situations (King & Armitage, 1958; Peters & Jenkins, 1954; Ullman et al., in press). These findings are particularly noteworthy since the response classes involved are similar to those psychotherapists are primarily concerned in modifying through interview forms of treatment. If the favorable results yielded by these studies are replicated in future investigations, it is likely that the next few years will witness an increasing reliance on conditioning forms of psychotherapy, particularly in the treatment of psychotic patients.

At this point it might also be noted that, consistent with the results from verbal conditioning experiments, content analyses of psychotherapeutic interviews (Bandura, Lipsher, & Miller, 1960; Murray, 1956) suggest that many of the changes observed in psychotherapy, at least insofar as the patients' verbal behavior is concerned, can be accounted for in terms of the therapists' direct, although usually unwitting, reward and punishment of the patients' expressions.

PUNISHMENT

While positive habits can be readily developed through reward, the elimination of socially disapproved habits, which becomes very much an issue in the treatment of antisocial personalities, poses a far more complex problem.

The elimination of socially disapproved behaviors can be accomplished in several ways. They may be consistently unrewarded and thus extinguished. However, antisocial behavior, particularly of an extreme form, cannot simply be ignored in the hope that it will gradually extinguish. Furthermore, since the successful execution of antisocial acts may bring substantial material rewards as well as the approval and admiration of associates, it is extremely unlikely that such behavior would ever extinguish. Although punishment may lead to the rapid disappearance of socially disapproved behavior, its effects are far more complex (Estes, 1944; Solomon, Kamin, & Wynne, 1953). If a person is punished for some socially disapproved habit, the impulse to perform the act becomes, through its association with punishment, a stimulus for anxiety. This anxiety then motivates competing responses which, if sufficiently strong, prevent the occurrence of, or inhibit, the disapproved behavior. Inhibited responses may not, however, thereby lose their strength, and may reappear in situations where the threat of punishment is weaker. Punishment may, in fact, prevent the extinction of a habit; if a habit is completely inhibited, it cannot occur and therefore cannot go unrewarded.

Several other factors point to the futility of punishment as a means of correcting many antisocial patterns. The threat of punishment is very likely to elicit conformity; indeed, the patient may obligingly do whatever he is told to do in order to avoid immediate difficulties. This does not mean, however, that he has acquired a set of sanctions that will be of service to him once he is outside the treatment situation. In fact, rather than leading to the development of internal controls, such methods are likely only to increase the patient's reliance on external restraints. Moreover, under these conditions, the majority of patients will develop the attitude that they will do only what they are told to do—and then often only half-heartedly—and that they will do as they please once they are free from the therapist's supervision (Bandura & Walters, 1959).

In addition, punishment may serve only to intensify hostility and other negative motivations and thus may further instigate the antisocial person to display the very behaviors that the punishment was intended to bring under control.

Mild aversive stimuli have been utilized, of course, in the treatment of voluntary patients who express a desire to rid themselves of specific debilitating conditions.

Liversedge and Sylvester (1955), for example, successfully treated seven cases of writer's cramp by means of a retraining procedure involving electric shock. In order to remove tremors, one component of the motor disorder, the patients were required to insert a stylus into a series of progressively smaller holes; each time the stylus made contact with the side of the hole the patients received a mild shock. The removal of the spasm component of the disorder was obtained in two ways. First, the patients traced various line patterns (similar to the movements required in writing) on a metal plate with a stylus, and any deviation from the path produced a shock. Following training on the apparatus, the subjects then wrote with an electrified pen which delivered a shock whenever excessive thumb pressure was applied.

Liversedge and Sylvester report that following the retraining the patients were able to resume work; a follow-up several months later indicated that the improvement was being maintained.

The aversive forms of therapy, described earlier in the section on counterconditioning procedures, also make use of mild punishment.

SOCIAL IMITATION

Although a certain amount of learning takes place through direct training and reward, a good deal of a person's behavior repertoire may be acquired through imitation of what he observes in others. If this is the case, social imitation may serve as an effective vehicle for the transmission of prosocial behavior patterns in the treatment of antisocial patients.

Merely providing a model for imitation is not, however, sufficient. Even though the therapist exhibits the kinds of behaviors that he wants the patient to learn, this is likely to have little influence on him if he rejects the therapist as a model. Affectional nurturance is believed to be an important precondition for imitative learning to occur, in that affectional rewards increase the secondary reinforcing properties of the model, and thus predispose the imitator to pattern his behavior after the rewarding person (Mowrer, 1950; Sears, 1957; Whiting, 1954). Some positive evidence for the influence of social rewards on imitation is provided by Bandura and Huston (in press) in a recent study of identification as a process of incidental imitation.

In this investigation preschool children performed an orienting task but, unlike most incidental learning studies, the experimenter performed the diverting task as well, and the extent to which the subjects patterned their behavior after that of the experimenter-model was measured.

A two-choice discrimination problem similar to the one employed by Miller and Dollard (1941) in their experiments of social imitation was used as the diverting task. On each trial, one of two boxes was loaded with two rewards (small multicolor pictures of animals) and the object of the game was to guess which box contained the stickers. The experimenter-model (M) always had her turn first and in each instance chose the reward box. During M's trial, the subject remained at the starting point where he could observe the M's behavior. On each discrimination trial M exhibited certain verbal, motor, and aggressive patterns of behavior that were totally irrelevant to the task to which the subject's attention was directed. At the starting point, for example, M made a verbal response and then marched slowly toward the box containing the stickers, repeating, "March, march, march." On the lid of each box was a rubber doll which M knocked off aggressively when she reached the designated box. She then paused briefly, remarked, "Open the box," removed one sticker, and pasted it on a pastoral scene which hung on the wall immediately behind the boxes. The subject then took his turn and the number of M's behaviors performed by the subject was recorded.

A control group was included in order to, (a) provide a check on whether the subjects' performances reflected genuine imitative learning or merely the chance occurrence of behaviors high in the subjects' response hierarchies, and (b) to determine whether subjects would adopt certain aspects of M's behavior which involved considerable delay in reward. With the controls, therefore, M walked to the box, choosing a highly circuitous route along the sides of the experimental room; instead of aggressing toward the doll, she lifted it gently off the container.

The results of this study indicate that, insofar as preschool children are concerned, a good deal of incidental imitation of the behaviors displayed by an adult model does occur. Of the subjects in the experimental group, 88% adopted the M's aggressive behavior, 44% imitated the marching, and 28% reproduced M's verbalizations. In contrast, none of the control subjects behaved aggressively, marched, or verbalized, while 75% of the controls imitated the circuitous route to the containers.

In order to test the hypothesis that children who experience a rewarding relationship with an adult model adopt more of the model's behavior than do children who experience a relatively distant and cold relationship, half the subjects in the experiment were assigned to a nurturant condition; the other half of the subjects to a nonnurturant condition.

During the nurturant sessions, which preceded the incidental learning, M played with subject, she responded readily to the subject's bids for attention, and in other ways fostered a consistently warm and rewarding interaction with the child. In contrast, during the nonnurturant sessions, the subject played alone while M busied herself with paperwork at a desk in the far corner of the room.

Consistent with the hypothesis, it was found that subjects who experienced the rewarding interaction with M adopted significantly more of M's behavior than did subjects who were in the nonnurturance condition.

A more crucial test of the transmission of behavior patterns through the process of social imitation involves the delayed generalization of imitative responses to new situations in which the model is absent. A study of this type just completed, provides strong evidence that observation of the cues produced by the behavior of others is an effective means of eliciting responses for which the original probability is very low (Bandura, Ross, & Ross, in press).

Empirical studies of the correlates of strong and weak identification with parents, lend additional support to the theory that rewards promote imitative learning. Boys whose fathers are highly rewarding and affectionate have been found to adopt the father-role in doll-play activities (Sears, 1953), to show father-son similarity in response to items on a personality questionnaire (Payne & Mussen, 1956), and to display masculine behaviors (Mussen & Distler, 1956, 1960) to a greater extent than boys whose fathers are relatively cold and non-rewarding.

The treatment of older unsocialized delinquents is a difficult task, since they are relatively self-sufficient and do not readily seek involvement with a therapist. In many cases, socialization can be accomplished only through residential care and treatment. In the treatment home, the therapist can personally administer many of the primary rewards and mediate between the boys' needs and gratifications. Through the repeated association with rewarding experiences for the boy, many of the therapist's attitudes and actions will acquire secondary reward value, and thus the patient will be motivated to reproduce these attitudes and actions in himself. Once these attitudes and values have been thus accepted, the boy's inhibition of antisocial tendencies will function independently of the therapist.

While treatment through social imitation has been suggested as a method for modifying antisocial patterns, it can be an effective procedure for the treatment of other forms of disorders as well. Jones (1924a), for example, found that the social example of children reacting normally to stimuli feared by another child was effective, in some instances, in eliminating such phobic reactions. In fact, next to counterconditioning, the method of social imitation proved to be most effective in eliminating inappropriate fears.

There is some suggestive evidence that by providing high prestige models and thus increasing the reinforcement value of the imitatee's behavior, the effectiveness of this method in promoting favorable adjustive patterns of behavior may be further increased (Jones, 1924a; Mausner, 1953, 1954; Miller & Dollard, 1941).

During the course of conventional psychotherapy, the patient is exposed to many incidental cues involving the therapist's values, attitudes, and patterns of behavior. They are incidental only because they are usually considered secondary or irrelevant to the task of resolving the patient's problems. Nevertheless, some of the changes observed in the patient's behavior may result, not so much from the intentional interaction between the patient and the therapist, but rather from active learning by the patient of the therapist's attitudes and values which the therapist never directly attempted to transmit. This is partially corroborated by Rosenthal (1955) who found that, in spite of the usual precautions taken by therapists to avoid imposing their values on their clients, the patients who were judged as showing the greatest improvement changed their moral values (in the areas of sex, aggression, and authority) in the direction of the values of their therapists, whereas patients who were unimproved became less like the therapist in values.

FACTORS IMPEDING INTEGRATION

In reviewing the literature on psychotherapy, it becomes clearly evident that learning theory and general psychology have exerted a remarkably minor influence on the practice of psychotherapy and, apart from the recent interest in Skinner's operant conditioning methods (Krasner, 1955; Skinner, 1953), most of the recent serious attempts to apply learning principles to clinical practice have been made by European psychotherapists (Jones, 1956; Lazarus & Rachman, 1957; Liversedge & Sylvester, 1955; Meyer, 1957; Rachman, 1959; Raymond, 1956; Wolpe, 1958; Yates, 1958). This isolation of the methods of treatment from our knowledge of learning and motivation will continue to exist for some time since there are several prevalent attitudes that impede adequate integration.

In the first place, the deliberate use of the principles of learning in the modification of human behavior implies, for most psychotherapists, manipulation and control of the patient, and control is seen by them as antihumanistic and, therefore, bad. Thus, advocates of a learning approach to psychotherapy are often charged with treating human beings as though they were rats or pigeons and of leading on the road to Orwell's 1984.

This does not mean that psychotherapists do not influence and control their patients' behavior. On the contrary. In any interpersonal interaction, and psychotherapy is no exception, people influence and control one another (Frank, 1959; Skinner, 1956a). Although the patient's control of the therapist has not as yet been studied (such control is evident when patients subtly reward the therapist with interesting historical material and thereby avoid the discussion of their current interpersonal problems), there is considerable evidence that the therapist exercises personal control over his patients. A brief examination of interview protocols of patients treated by therapists representing differing theoretical orientations, clearly reveals that the patients have been thoroughly conditioned in their therapists' idiosyncratic languages. Client-centered patients, for example, tend to produce the client-centered terminology, theory, and goals, and their interview content shows little or no overlap with that of patients seen in psychoanalysis who, in turn, tend to speak the language of psychoanalytic theory (Heine, 1950). Even more direct evidence of the therapists' controlling influence is provided in studies of patient-therapist interactions (Bandura et al., 1960; Murray, 1956; Rogers, 1960). The results of these studies show that the therapist not only controls the patient by rewarding him with interest and approval when the patient behaves in a fashion the therapist desires, but that he also controls through punishment, in the form of mild disapproval and withdrawal of interest, when the patient behaves in ways that are threatening to the therapist or run counter to his goals.

One difficulty in understanding the changes that occur in the course of psychotherapy is that the independent variable, i.e., the therapist's behavior, is often vaguely or only partially defined. In an effort to minimize or to deny the therapist's directive influence on the patient, the therapist is typically depicted as a "catalyst" who, in some mysterious way, sets free positive adjustive patterns of behavior or similar outcomes usually described in very general and highly socially desirable terms.

It has been suggested, in the material presented in the preceding sections, that many of the changes that occur in psychotherapy derive from the unwitting application of well-known principles of learning. However, the occurrence of the necessary conditions for learning is more by accident than by intent and, perhaps, a more deliberate application of our knowledge of the learning process to psychotherapy would yield far more effective results.

The predominant approach in the development of psychotherapeutic procedures has been the "school" approach. A similar trend is noted in the treatment methods being derived from learning theory. Wolpe, for example, has selected the principle of counterconditioning and built a "school" of psychotherapy around it; Dollard and Miller have focused on extinction and discrimination learning ; and the followers of Skinner rely almost entirely on methods of reward. This stress on a few learning principles at the expense of neglecting other relevant ones will serve only to limit the effectiveness of psychotherapy.

A second factor that may account for the discontinuity between general psychology and psychotherapeutic practice is that the model of personality to which most therapists subscribe is somewhat dissonant with the currently developing principles of behavior.

In their formulations of personality functioning, psychotherapists are inclined to appeal to a variety of inner explanatory processes, In contrast, learning theorists view the organism as a far more mechanistic and simpler system, and consequently their formulations tend to be expressed for the most part in terms of antecedent-consequent relationships without reference to inner states.
Symptoms are learned S-R connections; once they are extinguished or deconditioned treatment is complete. Such treatment is based exclusively on present factors; like Lewin's theory, this one is a-

historical. Nonverbal methods are favored over verbal ones, although a minor place is reserved for verbal methods of extinction and reconditioning. Concern is with function, not with content. The main difference between the two theories arises over the question of "symptomatic" treatment. According to orthodox theory, this is useless unless the underlying complexes are attacked. According to the present theory, there is no evidence for these putative complexes, and symptomatic treatment is all that is required (Eysenck, 1957, pp. 267-268). (Quoted by permission of Frederick A. Praeger, Inc.)

Changes in behavior brought about through such methods as counterconditioning are apt to be viewed by the "dynamically-oriented" therapist, as being not only superficial, "symptomatic" treatment, in that the basic underlying instigators of the behavior remain unchanged, but also potentially dangerous, since the direct elimination of a symptom may precipitate more seriously disturbed behavior.

This expectation receives little support from the generally favorable outcomes reported in the studies reviewed in this paper. In most cases where follow-up data were available to assess the long-term effects of the therapy, the patients, many of whom had been treated by conventional methods with little benefit, had evidently become considerably more effective in their social, vocational, and psychosexual adjustment. On the whole the evidence, while open to error, suggests that no matter what the origin of the maladaptive behavior may be, a change in behavior brought about through learning procedures may be all that is necessary for the alleviation of most forms of emotional disorders.

As Mowrer (1950) very aptly points out, the "symptom-underlying cause" formulation may represent inappropriate medical analogizing. Whether or not a given behavior will be considered normal or a symptom of an underlying disturbance will depend on whether or not somebody objects to the behavior. For example, aggressiveness on the part of children may be encouraged and considered a sign of healthy development by the parents, while the same behavior is viewed by school authorities and society as a symptom of a personality disorder (Bandura & Walters, 1959). Furthermore, behavior considered to be normal at one stage in development may be regarded as a "symptom of a personality disturbance" at a later period. In this connection it is very appropriate to repeat Mowrer's (1950) query: "And when does persisting behavior of this kind suddenly cease to be normal and become a symptom" (p. 474).

Thus, while a high fever is generally considered a sign of an underlying disease process regardless of when or where it occurs, whether a specific behavior will be viewed as normal or as a symptom of an underlying pathology is not independent of who makes the judgement, the social context in which the behavior occurs, the age of the person, as well as many other factors.

Another important difference between physical pathology and behavior pathology usually overlooked is that, in the case of most behavior disorders, it is not the underlying motivations that need to be altered or removed, but rather the ways in which the patient has learned to gratify his needs (Rotter, 1954). Thus, for example, if a patient displays deviant sexual behavior, the goal is not the removal of the underlying causes, i.e., sexual motivation, but rather the substitution of more socially approved instrumental and goal responses.

It might also be mentioned in passing, that, in the currently popular forms of psychotherapy, the role assumed by the therapist may bring him a good many direct or fantasized personal gratifications. In the course of treatment the patient may express considerable affection and admiration for the therapist, he may assign the therapist an omniscient status, and the reconstruction of the patient's history may be an intellectually stimulating activity. On the other hand, the methods derived from learning theory place the therapist in a less glamorous role, and this in itself may create some reluctance on the part of psychotherapists to part with the procedures currently in use.

Which of the two conceptual theories of personality - the psychodynamic or the social learning theory - is the more useful in generating effective procedures for the modification of human behavior remains to be demonstrated. While it is possible to present logical arguments and impressive clinical evidence for the efficiency of either approach, the best proving ground is the laboratory.

In evaluating psychotherapeutic methods, the common practice is to compare changes in a treated group with those of a nontreated control group. One drawback of this approach is that, while it answers the question as to whether or not a particular treatment is more effective than no intervention in producing changes along specific dimensions for certain classes of patients, it does not provide evidence concerning the relative effectiveness of alternative forms of psychotherapy.

It would be far more informative if, in future psychotherapy research, radically different forms of treatment were compared (King & Armitage, 1958; Rogers, 1959), since this approach would lead to a more rapid discarding of those of our cherished psychotherapeutic rituals that prove to be ineffective in, or even a handicap to, the successful treatment of emotional disorders.

REFERENCES

ADAMS, J. K. Laboratory studies of behavior without awareness. Psychol. Bull., 1957, 54, 393-405.

ALEXANDER, F, Psychoanalysis and psychotherapy. New York:

Norton, 1956. ALEXANDER, F., & FRENCH, M. T. Psychoanalytic therapy. New York: Ronald, 1946.

ATKINSON, RITA L. Paired-associate learning by schizophrenic and normal subjects under conditions of verbal reward and verbal punishment. Unpublished doctoral dissertation, Indiana University, 1957.

AZRAN, N. H., & LINDSLEY, O. R. The reinforcement of cooperation between children. J. abnorm. soc. Psychol., 1956, 52, 100-102.

BANDURA A., & HUSTON, ALETHA, C. Identification as a process of incidental learning. J. abnorm. soc. Psychol., in press.

BANDURA, A., LIPSHER, D. H., & MILLER, PAULA, E. Psychotherapists' approach avoidance reactions to patients' expressions of hostility. J. consult. Psychol., 1960, 24, 1-8.

BANDURA, A., Ross, DOROTHEA, & Ross, SHEILA, A. Transmission of aggression through imitation of aggressive models. J. abnorm. soc. Psychol., in press.

BANDURA, A., & WALTERS, R. H. Adolescent aggression. New York: Ronald, 1959.

CAIRNS, R. B. The influence of dependency anxiety on the effectiveness of social reinforcers. Unpublished doctoral dissertation, Stanford University, 1959.

CALVIN, A. D., CLIFFORD, L. T., CLIFFORD, B., BOLDEN, L., & HARVEY, J. Experimental validation of conditioned inhibition. Psychol. Rep., 1956, 2, 51-56.

DAVIDSON, J. R., & DOUGLASS, E. Nocturnal enuresis: A special approach to treatment. British med. J., 1950, 1, 1345-1347.

DITTES, J. E. Extinction during psychotherapy of GSR accompanying "embarrassing" statements. J. abnorm. soc. Psychol., 1957, 54, 187-191. (a)

DITTES, J. E. Galvanic skin responses as a measure of patient's reaction to therapist's permissiveness. J. abnorm. soc. Psychol., 1957, 55, 295-303. (b)

DOLLARD, J., AULD, F., & WHITE, A. M. Steps-in psychotherapy. New York: Macmillan, 1954. DOLLARD, J., & MILLER, N. E. Personality and psychotherapy. New York: McGraw-Hill, 1950.

DUNLAP, K. Habits, their making and unmaking. New York: Liveright, 1932.

EDMONSON, B. W., & AMSEL, A. The effects of massing and distribution of extinction trials on the persistence of a fear-motivated instrumental response. J. comp. physiol. Psychol., 1954, 47, 117-123.

ERIKSON, C. W. Unconscious processes. In M. R. Jones (Ed.), Nebraska symposium on motivation. Lincoln: Univer. Nebraska Press, 1958. ESTES, W. K. An experimental study of punishment. Psychol. Monogr., 1944, 57 (3, Whole No. 363).

EYSENCK, H. J. The dynamics of anxiety and hysteria. New York: Praeger, 1957. FENICHEL, O. Problems of psychoanalytic technique. (Trans, by D. Brunswick) New York: Psychoanalytic Quarterly, 1941.

FERSTER, C. B. Development of normal behavioral processes in autistic children. Res. relat. Child., 1959, No. 9, 30. (Abstract)

FISHMAN, H. C. A study of the efficiency of negative practice as a corrective for stammering. J. speech Dis., 1937, 2, 67-72.

FRANK, J. D. The dynamics of the psychotherapeutic relationship. Psychiatry, 1959, 22, 17-39.

FROMM-REICHMANN, FRIEDA. Principle of intensive psychotherapy. Chicago: Univer. Chicago Press, 1950.

HEINE, R. W. An investigation of the relationship between change in personality from psychotherapy as reported by patients and the factors seen by patients as producing change. Unpublished doctoral dissertation, University of Chicago, 1950,

JONES, E. L. Exploration of experimental extinction and spontaneous recovery in stuttering. In W. Johnson (Ed.), Stuttering in children and adults. Minneapolis: Univer. Minnesota Press, 1955.

JONES, H. G. The application of conditioning and learning techniques to the treatment of a psychiatric patient. J. abnorm. soc. Psychol., 1956, 52, 414-419. JONES, MARY C. The elimination of children's' fears. J. exp. Psychol., 1924, 7, 382-390. (a)

JONES, MARY C. A laboratory study of fear: The case of Peter. J. genet. Psychol, 1924, 31, 308-315. (b)

KING, G. F., & ARMITAGE, S. G. An operant interpersonal therapeutic approach to schizophrenics of extreme pathology. Amer. Psychologist, 1958, 13, 358. (Abstract)

KLEIN, MELANIE. The psycho-analysis of children. London: Hogarth, 1949.

KRASNER, L. The use of generalized reinforcers in psychotherapy research. Psychol. Rep., 1955, 1, 19-25.

KRASNER, L. Studies of the conditioning of verbal behavior. Psychol. Bull, 1958, 55, 148-170.

LACEY, J. I., & SMITH, R. I. Conditioning and generalization of unconscious anxiety. Science, 1954, 120, 1-8.

LAZARUS, A. A., & RACHMAN, S. The use of systematic desensitization in psychotherapy. S. Afr. med. J., 1957, 32, 934-937.

LEHNER, G. F. J. Negative practice as a psychotherapeutic technique. J. gen. Psychol., 1954, 51, 69-82.

LINDSLEY, O. R. Operant conditioning methods applied to research in chronic schizophrenia. Psychiat. res. Rep., 1956, 5, 118-138.

LIVERSEDGE, L. A., & SYLVESTER, J. D. Conditioning techniques in the treatment of writer's cramp. Lancet, 1955, 1, 1147-1149.

MARTIN, B., & KUELY, DELORES. Results of treatment of enuresis by a conditioned response method. J. consult. Psychol, 1955, 19, 71-73.

MAUSNER, B. Studies in social interaction: III. The effect of variation in one partner's prestige on the interaction of observer pairs. J. appl. Psychol, 1953, 37, 391-393.

MAUSNER, B. The effect of one partner's success in a relevant task on the interaction of observer pairs. J. abnorm. soc. Psychol, 1954, 49, 557-560.

MAX, L. W. Breaking up a homosexual fixation by the conditioned reaction technique: A case study. Psychol. Bull, 1935, 32, 734.
MEISSNER, J. H. The relationship between voluntary nonfluency and stuttering. J. speech Dis., 1946, 11, 13-33.

MEYER, V. The treatment of two phobic patients on the basis of learning principles: Case report. J. abnorm. soc. Psychol, 1957, 55, 261-266.

MILLER, N. E., & BOLLARD, J. Social learning and imitation. New Haven: Yale Univer. Press, 1941.

MORGAN, J. J. B., & WITHER, F. J. The treatment of enuresis by the conditioned reaction technique. J. genet. Psychol, 1939, 55, 59-65.

MOWRER, O, H. Learning theory and personality dynamics. New York: Ronald, 1950.

MOWRER, 0. H., & MOWRER ,W. M. Enuresis —a method for its study and treatment. Amer. J. Orthopsychiat., 1938, 8, 436-459.

MURRAY, E. J. The content-analysis method of studying psychotherapy. Psychol Monogr., 1956, 70 (13, Whole No. 420).

MUSSEN, P., & DISTLER, L. M. Masculinity, identification, and father-son relationships. J. abnorm. soc. Psychol, 1959, 59, 350-356.
MUSSEN, P., & DISTLER, L. M. Child-rearing antecedents of masculine identification in kindergarten boys. Child Develpm., 1960, 31, 89-100.

PAYNE, D. E., & MUSSEN, P. H. Parent-child relationships and father identification among adolescent boys. J. abnorm. soc. Psychol, 1956, 52, 358-362.

PETERS, H. N. Multiple choice learning in the chronic schizophrenic. J. din. Psychol, 1953, 9, 328-333.

PETERS, H. N., & JENKINS, R. L. Improvement of chronic schizophrenic patients with guided problem-solving motivated by hunger. Psychiat. Quart. Suppl, 1954, 28, 84-101.

RACHMAN, S. The treatment of anxiety and phobic reactions by systematic desensitization psychotherapy. J. abnorm. soc. Psychol, 1959, 58, 259-263.

RAYMOND, M. S. Case of fetishism treated by aversion therapy. Brit. med. J., 1956, 2, 854-857.

RAZRAN, G. Stimulus generalization of conditioned responses. Psychol Bull, 1949, 46, 337-365.

ROBINSON, NANCY M. Paired-associate learning by schizophrenic subjects under conditions of personal and impersonal reward and punishment. Unpublished doctoral dissertation, Stanford University, 1957.

ROGERS, C. R. Client-centered therapy. Boston: Houghton Mifflin, 1951.

ROGERS, C. R. Group discussion: Problems of controls. In E. H. Rubinstein & M. B, Parloff (Eds.), Research in psychotherapy. Washington, D. C.: American Psychological Association, 1959.

ROGERS, J. M, Operant conditioning in a quasi-therapy setting, J. abnorm. soc. Psychol., 1960, 60, 247-252.

ROSENTHAL, D, Changes in some moral values following psychotherapy. J. consult. Psychol, 1955, 19, 431-436.

ROTTER, J, B. Social learning and clinical psychology, Englewood Cliffs, N. J.: Prentice-Hall, 1954.

RUBENSTEIN, E. A., & LORR, M. A comparison of terminators and remainers in outpatient psychotherapy. J. din. Psychol., 1956, 12, 345-349.

RUTHERFORD, B. R. The use of negative practice in speech therapy with children handicapped by cerebral palsy, athetoid type. J. speech Dis,, 1940, 5, 259-264.

SALZINGER, K. Experimental manipulation of verbal behavior: A review. J. gen. Psychol., 1959, 61, 65-94.

SARASON, BARBARA R. The effects of verbally conditioned response classes on post-conditioning tasks. Dissertation Abstr., 1957, 12, 679.

SCHMIDBERG, MELITTA. Psychotherapy of juvenile delinquents. Int. ntent. hlth. res. Newsltr., 1959, 1, 1-2.

SEARS, PAULINE S. Child-rearing factors related to playing of sex-typed roles. Amer. Psychologist, 1953, 8, 431. (Abstract)

SEARS, R. R. Identification as a form of behavioral development. In D. B. Harris (Ed.), The concept of development: An issue in the study of human behavior. Minneapolis: Univer. Minnesota Press, 1957.

SHEEHAN, J. G. The modification of stuttering through non-reinforcement. J. abnorm. soc. Psychol, 1951, 46, 51-63.

SHEEHAN, J. G., & VOAS, R. B. Stuttering as conflict: I. Comparison of therapy techniques involving approach and avoidance. J. speech Dis., 1957, 22, 714-723.

SHOBEN, E. J. Psychotherapy as a problem in learning theory. Psychol. Bull, 1949, 46, 366-392.

SKINNER, B. F. Science and human behavior. New York: Macmillan, 1953.

SKINNER, B. F. Some issues concerning the control of human behavior. Science, 1956, 124, 1057-1066. (a)

SKINNER, B. F. What is psychotic behavior? In, Theory and treatment of psychosis: Some newer aspects. St. Louis: Washington Univer. Stud., 1956. (b)

SOLOMON, R. L., KAMIN, L. J., & WYNNE, L. C. Traumatic avoidance learning: The outcomes of several extinction procedures with dogs. J. abnorm. soc. Psychol., 1953, 48, 291-302.

SULLIVAN, H. S. The interpersonal theory of psychiatry. New York: Norton, 1953. THIRMANN, J. Conditioned-reflex treatment of alcoholism. NewEngl. J. Med., 1949,241, 368-370, 406-410.

THOMPSON, G. N., & BIELINSKI, B, Improvement in psychosis following conditioned reflex treatment in alcoholism. J. nerv. ment. Dis., 1953, 117, 537-543.

TILTON, J. R. The use of instrumental motor and verbal learning techniques in the treatment of chronic schizophrenics. Unpublished doctoral dissertation, Michigan State University, 1956.

ULLMAN, L. P., KRASNER, L., & COLLINS, Beverly J. Modification of behavior in group therapy associated with verbal conditioning. J, abnorm. soc. Psychol., in press.

VOEGTLEN, W. L. The treatment of alcoholism by establishing a conditioned reflex. Amer. J. med. Sci., 1940, 119, 802-810.

WALLACE, J. A. The treatment of alcoholics by the conditioned reflex method. J. Tenn. Med. Ass., 1949, 42, 125-128.

WEIDE, T. N. Conditioning and generalization of the use of affect-relevant words. Unpublished doctoral dissertation, Stanford University, 1959.

WHITING, J. W. M. The research program of the Laboratory of Human Development: The development of self-control. Cambridge: Harvard University, 1954. (Mimeo)

WILLIAMS, C. D. The elimination of tantrum behaviors by extinction procedures. J. abnorm. soc. Psychol., 1959, 59, 269.

WILLIAMS, R. I. Verbal conditioning in psychotherapy. Amer. Psychologist, 1959, 14, 388. (Abstract) WOLFE, J. Reciprocal inhibition as the main basis of psychotherapeutic effects. A MA Arch. Neural. Psychiat., 1954, 72, 205-226.

WOLPE, J. Psychotherapy by reciprocal inhibition. Stanford: Stanford Univer. Press, 1958.
WOLPE, J. Psychotherapy based on the principle of reciprocal inhibition. In A. Burton (Ed.), Case studies in counseling and psychotherapy. Englewood Cliffs, N. J.: Prentice-Hall, 1959.

YATES, A. J. The application of learning theory to the treatment of tics. J. abnorm. soc. Psychol, 1958, 56, 175-182.

7. READ MORE PSYCHOLOGY CLASSICS

Superstition in the Pigeon

Burrhus Frederic "B. F." Skinner ranks among the most frequently cited and influential psychologists in the history of the discipline. Building on the behaviorist theories of Ivan Pavlov and John Watson he was the first psychologist to receive a Lifetime Achievement Award from the American Psychological Association (APA.) Originally published in 1948, Superstition in The Pigeon is a learning theory classic.

You can get hold of Superstition in The Pigeon via the following Amazon website link.

www.amazon.com/dp/B00DL6HL3Y

Transmission of Aggression Through Imitation of Aggressive Models: The Bobo Doll Experiment

Albert Bandura is one the world's most frequently cited psychologists. His ground-breaking work within the field of social learning and social cognitive theory led to a paradigm shift within psychology away from psychodynamic and behaviorist perspectives. As part of a new research agenda in the early 1960's which posited that people learn vicariously through observation Bandura began investigating aggression through imitation; work that gave rise to one of the most famous psychology studies of all time, "Transmission of Aggression Through Imitation of Aggressive Models." More commonly known as "The Bobo Doll Experiment," it was the first study to explore the impact of televised violence on children.

You can get hold of Transmission of Aggression Through Imitation of Aggressive Models: The Bobo Doll Experiment via the following Amazon website link.

www.amazon.com/dp/B00DHDC7Z8

Conditioned Emotional Reactions: The Case of Little Albert

Conditioned Emotional Reactions by John B. Watson and Rosalie Rayner is one of the most influential, infamous and iconic research articles ever published in the history of psychology. Commonly referred to as "The Case of Little Albert" this psychology classic attempted to show how fear could be induced in an infant through classical conditioning. Originally published in 1920, Conditioned Emotional Reactions remains among the most frequently cited journal articles in introductory psychology courses and textbooks.

One of the most dramatic aspects of Watson and Rayner's original study was that they had planned to test a number of methods by which they could remove Little Albert's conditioned fear responses. However, as Watson noted "Unfortunately Albert was taken from the hospital the day the above tests were made. Hence the opportunity of building up an experimental technique by means of which we could remove the conditioned emotional responses was denied us."

This unforeseen turn of events was something that obviously stayed with Watson, as under his guidance some three years later, Mary Cover Jones conducted a follow-up study - A Laboratory Study of Fear: The Case of Peter - which illustrated how fear may be removed under laboratory conditions. This additional and highly relevant article is also presented in full.

You can get hold of Conditioned Emotional Reactions: The Case of Little Albert via the following Amazon website link.

www.amazon.com/dp/B00BOVL3TQ

Hierarchy of Needs: A Theory of Human Motivation

A Theory of Human Motivation by Abraham H. Maslow is one of the most famous psychology articles ever written. Originally published in 1943, it was in this landmark paper that Maslow presented his first detailed representation of Self-Actualization - the desire to become everything that one is capable of becoming - at the pinnacle of a hierarchy of human needs.

In A Theory of Human Motivation Maslow draws upon some of his earlier published work. Three of these key references, Conflict, Frustration And The Theory of Threat, The Dynamics of Psychological Security-Insecurity and Preface To Motivation Theory are also presented in full.

You can get hold of Hierarchy of Needs: A Theory of Human Motivation via the following Amazon website link.

www.amazon.com/dp/B004JKMUKU

8. CONNECT AND LEARN

Join thousands of psychology enthusiasts online.

Psychology on Facebook

www.facebook.com/psychologyonline

Psychology on Twitter

twitter.com/psych101

Psychology on Google+

goo.gl/hU8JL

Psychology on Linkedin

www.linkedin.com/groups/Psychology-Students-Network-4016322/about

Psychology on YouTube

www.youtube.com/user/LearnAboutPsychology

Psychology on Pinterest

pinterest.com/psychology

Psychology Student Guide

The Psychology Student Guide is designed for anyone who would like to learn more about what psychology actually is; anyone who is thinking about studying the subject or anyone who is currently a psychology student. See following Amazon website link for full details.

www.amazon.com/dp/B009ZC2UOS

The "ALL ABOUT" Website Portfolio

www.all-about-psychology.com

www.all-about-forensic-psychology.com

www.all-about-forensic-science.com

www.all-about-body-language.com